# *Fast* and *Fabulous*

# Fast and Fabulous

## MEALS FOR BUSY PEOPLE

The Australian Women's Weekly cookbooks

# Contents

## Special Features

# Time-saving Tips

### Think ahead

Planning is the key to saving time in the kitchen. Work out what you're going to eat for the coming week, buy all your dry and canned ingredients (fresh meat, fish, fruit and vegetables can be bought as you need them) and do as much preparation as you can in advance.

Sauces can be cooked and refrigerated or frozen, and meat and fish can be marinated overnight ready to quickly stir-fry the next night. A well-planned weekly menu will save you hours every week.

### Plan B

Not everyone is this well-organised, so here are some suggestions for the more haphazard cook.

• Keep your store cupboard well-stocked with staples (see opposite). If you have the makings

of a simple pasta dish or a vegetable curry always on hand, you can keep your family well-fed and happy.

• Make sure you have supplies of fast-cooking polenta, couscous and noodles so you can knock up a side dish in no time at all.

• Get to know stir-fries (and invest in a wok). You can make a delicious and nutritious stir-fry for four in under 15 minutes. And the more you use this method of cooking, the more you'll experiment with different flavours, expanding your repertoire and increasing your enjoyment.

• Buy tender, choice cuts of meat. These may seem extravagant at first, but if time is short, you'll see what a saving it is to buy quick-cooking meat. You'll spend less time trimming fat and gristle from it too.

• Eat more fish. Fish cutlets, and especially fillets, cook very

quickly and fish is a healthy low-fat food. Fish doesn't have to be fried or grilled. Try a casserole of fish, cooked in a tomato and vegetable sauce and served with bread. (The sauce can be made in advance and all you have to do is heat it up, add chopped fish, cook for a few minutes and serve sprinkled with parsley.)

• Keep dried herbs in the pantry to use when you can't get fresh. 1 teaspoon of dried herbs is equivalent to one tablespoon fresh.

• Use packaged products judiciously. Bottled tomato pasta sauce, curry pastes, minced ginger, etc. are all time-savers and many are of very good quality. Read labels carefully before you buy to make sure you're not buying a jar of preservatives.

### The microwave

Use your microwave oven to defrost frozen food, to reheat casseroles and other cooked food, and to cook vegetables and fish.

Meals for one or two can be very quickly cooked in the microwave — a baked potato takes 4-6 minutes, instead of the usual hour in the oven. But cooking rice or pasta for four people in the microwave takes about the same time as it does in a saucepan on the stove.

## Pantry basics

A supply of staples — tinned, bottled and frozen foods — will mean that even if you didn't have time to shop at lunchtime you'll still be able to produce a tasty meal for dinner.

artichoke hearts, bottled
breadcrumbs
butter beans, canned
Cajun seasoning
cannellini beans, canned
chickpeas, canned
chilli powder
chilli sauce
cinnamon sticks
corn kernels, canned
creamed corn, canned

coconut cream and milk
coriander, ground
corn chips
cornflour
couscous
cumin, ground
curry pastes
curry powder
flour, plain
garam masala
ginger, ground
herbs, dried
honey
kidney beans, canned
lentils, red
mango chutney
mustard
noodles
nutmeg, ground
oil (olive, vegetable)
olives, black

oyster sauce
pasta
rice (long-grain, arborio)
salmon, canned
sambal oelek
satay sauce
sesame seeds
soy sauce
stocks
sugar (white, brown)
sun-dried tomatoes
paprika, sweet
Tabasco sauce
tandoori paste
tomatoes, canned
tomato paste
tomato pasta sauce
tuna, canned
turmeric, ground
vinegar (balsamic, wine)
wine

*Refrigerator*
butter, margarine
cheese
cream
eggs
milk
sour cream
yogurt

*Freezer*
bacon
bread
breadcrumbs, stale
pine nuts
pizza bases

*Fruit and vegetables*
carrots
chillies
garlic
ginger
lemons, limes
potatoes

## Freezing food

One of the best ways to save time in the kitchen is to cook twice as much as you need for one dish, and freeze the rest. You can't freeze everything of course, but most casseroles, pies, sauces and soups freeze very well and taste just as good (curries taste even better) when reheated.

• Label and date everything you freeze.

• Freeze lemon and lime juice in ice-cube containers then re-package in freezer bags. Do the same with stock, and drop one or two cubes as required into sauces, soups and vegetable dishes for extra flavour.

• Milk, bread, butter and cream can all be frozen. Cut butter into portions before freezing.

• Leftover cooked rice and cooked dried (not fresh) pasta freeze very well.

• Chop and fry about 8 onions and 8 cloves of garlic in olive oil; divide among four small plastic bags. They don't freeze solid so you can just drop the contents into a frying pan and take it from there.

• Freeze fresh herbs, chillies, lemon grass and ginger either dry in freezer bags or finely chopped in ice-cube trays, barely covered with water. Wash and dry the herbs well first; peel and chop the lemon grass; and peel the ginger but freeze in pieces — it grates more easily when frozen. Transfer the frozen cubes to freezer bags for storage.

• Store prawn shells and other offensive-smelling rubbish such as meat scraps in the freezer until garbage collection.

# Chicken

# Chicken with thyme butter sauce

**PREPARATION TIME** 5 minutes
**COOKING TIME** 20 minutes

|   |   |
|---|---|
| 4 | chicken breast fillets (680g) |
|   | plain flour |
| ¼ | cup (60ml) olive oil |
| 125g | butter |
| 1 | tablespoon chopped fresh thyme |
| 2 | green onions, chopped |
| ¼ | cup (60ml) lemon juice |

Toss chicken in flour, shake away excess flour. Heat oil and half the butter in large frying pan, add chicken to pan, cook over medium heat for about 10 minutes or until tender. Drain chicken on absorbent paper, keep warm. Discard pan juices.

Heat remaining butter in same pan, add thyme and green onions, stir over medium heat for about 2 minutes or until green onions are soft. Stir in juice, cook over medium heat for 3 minutes. Serve chicken with zucchini if desired. Drizzle with sauce.

**SERVES 4**

**Per Serving** 48.7g fat; 2485kJ
**Store** Best made close to serving time.
**Microwave** Microwave chicken on HIGH for about 8 minutes. Cook butter, thyme and green onions on HIGH for about 2 minutes. Add juice and cook on HIGH for 3 minutes.

# Chicken with almond sauce

**PREPARATION TIME** 15 minutes
**COOKING TIME** 25 minutes

¼ cup (60ml) olive oil
½ cup (125ml) orange juice
3 cloves garlic, crushed
6 single chicken breast fillets (1kg)
3 small fennel bulbs (900g)
2 medium red onions (340g)
1 tablespoon olive oil, extra

Almond Sauce

1 tablespoon olive oil
¼ cup (15g) stale breadcrumbs
¾ cup (90g) ground almonds
  pinch ground cloves
1 cup (250ml) chicken stock
2 tablespoons dry white wine
¼ cup (60ml) thickened cream

Combine oil, juice, garlic and chicken in a medium bowl; brush over chicken

Cook chicken on a heated oiled grill pan until browned both sides and cooked through. Meanwhile, cut fennel and onions into wedges. Heat extra oil in large frying pan, add fennel and onions; cook, stirring, until onions are soft and lightly browned. Remove from heat, cover to keep warm. Serve chicken with fennel mixture and Almond Sauce.

**Almond sauce** Heat oil in medium frying pan, add breadcrumbs, cook, stirring, until lightly browned. Add almonds and cloves; cook, stirring, until lightly browned. Gradually add combined stock and wine, stir over heat until mixture is smooth; bring to boil. Remove from heat, stir in cream.

**SERVES 6**

**Per Serving** 36.8g fat; 2289kJ
**Store** Best made close to serving time.

# Saucy chicken in yogurt

**PREPARATION TIME**
10 minutes (plus standing time)

**COOKING TIME** 20 minutes

- 750g   chicken tenderloins
- 525g   bottled satay sauce
-    2   large brown onions (400g)
-    1   tablespoon olive oil
- 250g   cherry tomatoes, halved
- $1/3$   cup shredded fresh basil leaves
- 200ml  plain yogurt
-    2   tablespoons sweet chilli sauce

Combine chicken and $1/2$ cup (125ml) of the satay sauce in large bowl; stand 5 minutes.

Cook chicken, in batches, in large heated oiled frying pan until cooked through. Cover to keep warm.

Meanwhile, cut onions into wedges. Heat oil in same pan; cook onion, stirring, until soft. Add remaining satay sauce, tomatoes and basil; cook, stirring, about 5 minutes or until heated through.

Return chicken to pan; stir to coat with satay sauce mixture. Serve chicken with combined yogurt and chilli sauce.

**SERVES 4**

**Per Serving** 48.3g fat; 3456kJ

**Store** Chicken can be marinated several hours or overnight. Cook close to serving time.

**Microwave** Microwave chicken on HIGH for about 5 minutes. Cook onion, satay sauce, tomatoes and basil on HIGH for about 2 minutes. Return chicken to dish and cook on HIGH for 2 minutes.

# Chicken salad with tarragon coconut dressing

**PREPARATION TIME** 20 minutes
**COOKING TIME** 5 minutes

1.2kg  barbecued chicken
   3  bacon rashers, chopped
   1  small red onion (100g), chopped
   1  medium avocado (250g), chopped
250g  punnet cherry tomatoes
   1  small green cucumber (130g), chopped
  1/3  cup (50g) pimiento-stuffed green olives, halved
   1  cos lettuce

**Tarragon Coconut Dressing**

  1  teaspoon chopped fresh tarragon
  3  teaspoons tomato paste
  2  teaspoons sambal oelek
1/2  teaspoon sugar
1/4  cup (60ml) coconut cream
1/3  cup (80ml) peanut oil

Remove skin and bones from chicken; chop chicken. Cook bacon in small frying pan over medium heat until lightly browned; drain on absorbent paper.

Combine chicken, bacon, onion, avocado, tomato, cucumber and olives in large bowl. Place lettuce leaves in salad bowl, top with chicken mixture. Pour dressing over salad just before serving.

**Tarragon coconut dressing** Blend or process tarragon, paste, sambal oelek, sugar and cream until combined. With motor operating, gradually add oil in a thin stream, blend until mixture is thick.

**SERVES 6**

**Per Serving** 28g fat; 1545kJ
**Store** Salad and dressing can be made a day ahead; keep, covered, in refrigerator.
**Microwave** Microwave bacon on HIGH for 2 minutes or until crisp

# Lemon chicken parcels

**PREPARATION TIME**
15 minutes (plus cooling time)
**COOKING TIME** 30 minutes

30g  butter
  1  tablespoon vegetable oil
  4  chicken breast fillets (680g)
  8  sheets fillo pastry
60g  butter, melted, extra
  1  tablespoon seeded mustard
  1  tablespoon chopped fresh coriander

Lemon Sauce

  1  tablespoon lemon juice
  1  tablespoon chopped fresh coriander
  1  tablespoon grated fresh ginger
  ½  cup (125ml) thickened cream

Heat butter and oil in a medium frying pan, add chicken, cook both sides until lightly browned. Remove from pan, drain and cool. Reserve the frying pan with juices for sauce.

To prevent fillo from drying out, cover with damp tea-towel until ready to use. Place 1 sheet of fillo on bench, brush with some of the extra butter. Top with another layer of fillo, brush with butter. Fold fillo in half, place a chicken fillet in centre of 1 end of fillo. Spread chicken with some of the mustard and sprinkle with a little coriander. Fold sides of fillo over chicken, roll up to form a parcel. Repeat with remaining fillo, butter, chicken, mustard and coriander.

Place chicken parcels on greased oven tray, brush with remaining extra butter. Bake, uncovered, in moderate oven 20 minutes or until golden. Serve with Lemon Sauce. Accompany with boiled new potatoes and asparagus, if desired.

**Lemon sauce** Add all ingredients to the reserved juices in the frying pan. Stir constantly over heat until reduced by half.

**SERVES 4**

**Per Serving** 44.9g fat; 2725kJ
**Store** Parcels can be prepared several hours ahead; keep, covered, in refrigerator.

# Barbecue-flavoured chicken and onions

**PREPARATION TIME** 10 minutes
**COOKING TIME** 20 minutes

   2 **tablespoons lemon juice**
   2 **tablespoons brown sugar**
   1 **tablespoon honey**
   1 **clove garlic, crushed**
¼ **cup (60ml) soy sauce**
   2 **medium brown onions (300g)**
1.6kg **barbecued chicken, quartered**

Combine juice, sugar, honey, garlic and sauce in small jug. Chop onions into wedges. Place chicken and onion in shallow baking dish; pour over half the glaze mixture.

Bake, uncovered, in moderately hot oven about 20 minutes or until chicken is crisp and heated through, brushing frequently with remaining glaze mixture.

**SERVES 4**

**Per Serving** 14.3g fat;1291kJ
**Store** Dish can be made a day ahead; keep, covered, in refrigerator.

# Chicken and lemon grass stir-fry

**PREPARATION TIME** 15 minutes
**COOKING TIME** 15 minutes

  2 **tablespoons peanut oil**
  1 **teaspoon sesame oil**
¼ **cup chopped fresh lemon grass**
  1 **clove garlic, crushed**
  1 **birdseye chilli, chopped**
  4 **chicken breast fillets (680g), chopped**
  2 **teaspoons cornflour**
¼ **cup (60ml) water**
  1 **tablespoon fish sauce**
  1 **tablespoon oyster sauce**
½ **teaspoon sugar**
½ **x 230g can water chestnuts, chopped**
  1 **medium green capsicum (200g), sliced**

Heat oils in wok or large frying pan, add lemon grass, garlic and chilli, stir-fry for 1 minute. Add chicken, stir-fry in 2 batches for about 4 minutes or until tender. Blend cornflour with water, stir into chicken mixture with sauces and sugar. Stir over high heat until mixture boils and thickens. Stir in chestnuts and capsicum, stir over medium heat a further minute.

**SERVES 4**

Per Serving 19.9g fat; 1480kJ
Store Best made close to serving time.

# Kebabs with chilli garlic mayonnaise

**PREPARATION TIME** 35 minutes
**COOKING TIME** 10 minutes

500g  chicken thigh fillets
   1  teaspoon finely grated lime rind
 ¼  cup (60ml) lime juice
   1  tablespoon olive oil

Chilli Garlic Mayonnaise

   1  egg yolk
   2  cloves garlic, crushed
   2  tablespoons lime juice
   2  tablespoons sweet chilli sauce
   1  cup (250ml) peanut oil
   1  tablespoon coarsely chopped
       fresh coriander

Cut chicken into 3 cm cubes; thread onto
8 skewers. Combine rind, juice and oil in a
shallow dish, add skewers, turn skewers to
coat well, cover; stand 10 minutes.

Cook skewers, in batches, brushing with
marinade on heated oiled grill plate (or grill
or barbecue) until browned all over.

Serve kebabs with Chilli Garlic Mayonnaise.

**Chilli garlic mayonnaise** Blend or process
egg yolk, garlic, juice and sauce until
smooth. With motor operating, gradually add
the oil in a thin stream, blend until thick. Stir
in coriander.

**SERVES 4**

Per serving 74.2g fat; 3239kJ
**Store** Kebabs can be marinated and mayonnaise
can be made a day ahead; store, covered, in
refrigerator.

# Chicken and corn with egg rolls

**PREPARATION TIME** 10 minutes
**COOKING TIME** 20 minutes

   2 **eggs**
   1 **tablespoon peanut oil**
130g **can creamed corn**
   1 **tablespoon chopped fresh ginger**
   1 **clove garlic, crushed**
   1 **birdseye chilli, seeded, chopped**
   1 **small white onion (80g), chopped**
  ½ **cup (125ml) chicken stock**
700g **chicken thigh fillets**
100g **fresh baby corn**
   1 **medium red capsicum (200g), sliced**
   6 **green onions, sliced**

Whisk eggs and 1 teaspoon of the oil in small jug.

Brush heated wok with a little of the oil; add half of the egg mixture, swirling wok to form a thin omelette. Remove omelette from wok; repeat with remaining egg mixture.

Roll omelettes tightly; cut into thin slices.

Blend or process creamed corn, ginger, garlic, chilli, white onion and stock until almost smooth.

Cut each chicken fillet into thirds.

Heat remaining oil in same wok; stir-fry chicken, in batches, until browned and cooked through.

Stir-fry baby corn and capsicum in same wok until just tender.

Return chicken to wok with creamed corn mixture; stir-fry until sauce boils.

Add green onion and egg roll slices; stir-fry, tossing to combine ingredients.

**SERVES 4**

**Per Serving** 20.6g fat; 1652kJ
**Store** Best made close to serving time.
**Microwave** Microwave egg mixture on MEDIUM for 1 minute.

# Sesame chicken with choy sum

**PREPARATION TIME**
10 minutes (plus standing time)

**COOKING TIME** 10 minutes

700g    chicken breast fillets, sliced thinly
   2    cloves garlic, crushed
   1    tablespoon grated lemon rind
   1    cup (150g) plain flour, approximately
   2    eggs, beaten lightly
   1    cup (150g) white sesame seeds
  1/3    cup (80ml) peanut oil
250g    choy sum, chopped

Combine chicken with garlic and rind in large bowl; cover, refrigerate 10 minutes.

Dip chicken in flour, shake away excess; dip chicken in egg then, using your hands, press on seeds. Place chicken on tray, cover, refrigerate 20 minutes.

Heat oil in wok; stir-fry chicken, in batches, until browned and cooked through. Drain on absorbent paper.

Return chicken to wok with choy sum; stir-fry, tossing, until choy sum just wilts.

Serve with lemon wedges, if desired.

**SERVES 4**

**Per Serving** 52g fat; 3323kJ
**Store** Chicken can be marinated several hours or overnight; keep, covered, in refrigerator. Best cooked just before serving time.

# Chicken and pasta salad

**PREPARATION TIME**
20 minutes (plus cooling time)
**COOKING TIME** 10 minutes

      2  **chicken breast fillets (340g)**
220g **fettuccine**
100g **snow peas**
125g **broccoli**
      2  **teaspoons sesame seeds, toasted**
      1  **medium green capsicum (200g), sliced**
      6  **green onions, chopped**

## Dressing

      1/4 **cup (60ml) lemon juice**
      1  **tablespoon French mustard**
      1  **tablespoon chopped fresh parsley**
      2  **teaspoons grated fresh ginger**
      1/4 **cup (60ml) water**

Poach, steam or microwave chicken until tender; drain, cool, slice finely.

Add fettuccine to large saucepan of boiling water, boil, uncovered, for 10 minutes or until just tender; drain. Rinse fettuccine under cold water; drain.

Drop snow peas and broccoli into small saucepan of boiling water, return to boil, drain, place into bowl of iced water; drain.

Place fettuccine on serving plate, top with snow peas, broccoli, capsicum, green onions and chicken, sprinkle with sesame seeds. Add Dressing just before serving.

**Dressing** Combine all ingredients in a screw-top jar; shake well.

## SERVES 4

**Per Serving** 6.6g fat; 1431kJ
**Store** Chicken, snow peas and broccoli can be prepared several hours ahead; keep, covered, in refrigerator. Dressing can be made several days ahead; keep, covered, in refrigerator.

# Mango chicken with spinach and kumara

**PREPARATION TIME** 10 minutes
**COOKING TIME** 20 minutes

1/4 **cup (60ml) peanut oil**
500g **kumara, sliced**
750g **minced chicken**
1 **medium white onion (150g), chopped**
1 **clove garlic, crushed**
1 **tablespoon ground cumin**
1/3 **cup (90g) mango chutney**
2 **tablespoons lime juice**
150g **snow peas, halved**
250g **spinach, trimmed, chopped**

Heat half the oil in wok; stir-fry kumara, in batches, until just tender.

Heat remaining oil in wok; stir-fry chicken with onion, garlic and cumin, in batches, until chicken is browned and cooked through.

Return chicken mixture and kumara to wok with remaining ingredients; stir-fry, tossing, until spinach is just wilted.

**SERVES 4**

**Per Serving** 29.6g fat; 2351kJ
**Store** Best made close to serving time.

# Chilli coconut chicken curry

**PREPARATION TIME** 15 minutes
**COOKING TIME** 15 minutes

**30g butter**
   3 **chicken thigh fillets (about 330g), sliced**
   1 **large brown onion (200g), sliced**
   1 **clove garlic, crushed**
   1 **tablespoon chopped fresh lemon grass**
  ½ **teaspoon red chilli flakes**
   2 **teaspoons chopped fresh coriander**
   2 **teaspoons lime juice**
  ½ **teaspoon cumin seeds**
  ½ **teaspoon turmeric**
  ½ **teaspoon fish sauce**
   1 **teaspoon sugar**
   2 **teaspoons plain flour**
  ¾ **cup (180ml) coconut milk**

Heat butter in pan, add chicken, cook, stirring, until browned and tender; drain on absorbent paper.

Reheat pan, add onion, garlic, lemon grass, chilli, coriander, juice, seeds, turmeric and fish sauce; cook, stirring, until onion is soft. Stir in chicken, sugar and flour, then milk, stir over heat until mixture boils and thickens. Serve with brown rice and baked kumara, if desired.

**SERVES 4**

**Per Serving** 21.6g fat; 1214kJ
**Store** Recipe can be made 3 hours ahead; keep, covered, in refrigerator.

# Creamy chicken and asparagus pastries

**PREPARATION TIME**
20 minutes (plus cooling time)
**COOKING TIME** 40 minutes

*You will need ²/3 cup (130g) raw rice to make this dish.*

- 3 **sheets ready-rolled puff pastry**
- 1 **egg yolk**
- 1 **tablespoon milk**
- 2 **teaspoons sesame seeds**

**Filling**

- 1 **tablespoon olive oil**
- 400g **chicken thigh fillets, sliced**
- 1 **small leek (200g), sliced**
- 250g **asparagus, chopped**
- 2 **cups cooked white long-grain rice**
- ½ **cup (125ml) cream**
- 2 **teaspoons French mustard**
- 1 **teaspoon chopped fresh thyme**
- ¼ **cup (60ml) cream, extra**

Cut each sheet of pastry in half diagonally. Place one-sixth of the filling in centre of each triangle. Brush edges of pastry with some of the combined egg yolk and milk, fold pastry over filling to form a triangle, press edges together to seal.

Place pastries on greased oven tray, brush with more combined egg yolk and milk, sprinkle with seeds. Bake in hot oven 10 minutes, reduce heat to moderately hot, bake 10 minutes or until browned.

**Filling** Heat oil in pan, add chicken, cook, stirring, until browned. Add leek, cook, stirring, until leek is soft. Stir in asparagus, rice, cream, mustard and thyme, stir over heat until asparagus is just tender and mixture is thick, stir in extra cream; cool.

**MAKES 6**

Per Pastry 27.7g fat; 1800kJ
**Store** Filling can be made a day ahead; keep, covered, in refrigerator.

# Chicken Tuscany

**PREPARATION TIME** 10 minutes
**COOKING TIME** 15 minutes

700g chicken breast fillets, sliced thinly
  ½ teaspoon sweet paprika
  ¼ cup (60ml) olive oil
  2 medium brown onions (300g), sliced
  3 cloves garlic, crushed
  2 medium tomatoes (380g), seeded, sliced
  1 tablespoon drained capers
  2 tablespoons tomato paste
  ¼ cup (60ml) dry white wine
  ¼ cup (60ml) chicken stock
500g frozen broad beans, cooked, peeled
  ¼ cup firmly packed fresh basil leaves
  ⅓ cup (90g) black olive paste
  ¼ cup (20g) flaked parmesan cheese

Combine chicken and paprika in large bowl.

Heat 1 tablespoon of the oil in wok; stir-fry chicken, onion and garlic, in batches, until chicken is browned and cooked through.

Heat remaining oil in wok; stir-fry tomato and capers until tender.

Return chicken to wok with combined paste, wine and stock; stir-fry until sauce boils.

Add broad beans and basil to wok; stir-fry, tossing until hot.

Serve chicken mixture topped with olive paste and cheese.

**SERVES 4**

**Per Serving** 25.9g fat; 2137kJ
**Store** Best made close to serving time.

# Pesto-grilled chicken drumsticks

**PREPARATION TIME** 10 minutes
**COOKING TIME** 15 minutes

*We used a sun-dried tomato pesto in this recipe but you might prefer to experiment with one of the other different flavours.*

| | |
|---|---|
| 12 | chicken drumsticks (1.8kg) |
| 1 | tablespoon olive oil |
| 2 | tablespoons lemon juice |
| 3 | cloves garlic, crushed |
| 125g | butter, softened |
| 2 | tablespoons bottled pesto |

Make deep diagonal cuts across each chicken drumstick. Combine oil, juice and garlic in large bowl; add chicken, coat with oil mixture.

Combine butter and pesto in small bowl; press two-thirds of the pesto mixture into cuts and all over chicken.

Cook chicken under heated grill, brushing with remaining pesto mixture occasionally, until browned all over and cooked through. Brush chicken with pan juices and serve.

**SERVES 4**

**Per Serving** 43.8g fat; 2213kJ
**Store** Chicken can be cooked a day ahead; keep, covered, in refrigerator. Serve hot or cold.

# Marinated chicken and tomato kebabs

**PREPARATION TIME**
10 minutes (plus cooling time)
**COOKING TIME** 10 minutes

       9  chicken thigh fillets (1kg)
     ¼  cup (60ml) lime juice
     ¼  cup (60ml) olive oil
     ¼  cup chopped fresh garlic chives
     ¼  cup chopped fresh mint
       2  teaspoons sambal oelek
       2  teaspoons sugar
       2  teaspoons cracked black peppercorns
  500g  cherry tomatoes, halved
  330g  yellow teardrop tomatoes, halved

**Minted Lime Sauce**

     ½  cup (125ml) white wine vinegar
       2  green onions, chopped
       2  bay leaves
       6  black peppercorns
     ¼  cup (60ml) lime juice
       4  egg yolks
  250g  butter, melted
       2  medium tomatoes (380g),
            seeded, chopped
       2  teaspoons grated lime rind
       2  tablespoons chopped fresh mint

Cut chicken into 3cm pieces. Combine chicken, juice, oil, chives, mint, sambal oelek, sugar and pepper in medium bowl; mix well. Cover, refrigerate 10 minutes.

Thread chicken and tomatoes onto 18 skewers. Cook skewers in batches in heated greased

grill pan (or grill or barbecue) until chicken is tender. Serve with Minted Lime Sauce.

**Minted lime sauce** Combine vinegar, green onions, bay leaves, peppercorns and juice in small pan; simmer, uncovered, about 5 minutes or until reduced to 2 tablespoons, strain; discard onion mixture. Whisk vinegar mixture and egg yolks in medium bowl until creamy, gradually whisk in hot butter until mixture is thick. Stir in tomatoes, rind and mint.

**MAKES 18**

Per Kebab 19.8g fat; 975kJ
**Store** Chicken can be mari  .ed several hours or overnight; keep, covered, i. refrigerator. Cook just before serving time.

# Light and spicy crumbed chicken

**PREPARATION TIME**
10 minutes (plus standing time)
**COOKING TIME** 15 minutes

12  chicken tenderloins (900g)
⅓  cup (50g) plain flour
 2  egg whites, beaten lightly
⅓  cup (35g) packaged breadcrumbs
⅓  cup (35g) Corn Flake crumbs
 2  teaspoons garlic salt
 1  teaspoon lemon pepper

Toss chicken in flour; shake away excess flour. Coat chicken in egg whites, then in combined breadcrumbs, Corn Flake crumbs, salt and pepper. Cover, refrigerate 15 minutes.

Place chicken in single layer on oven tray; bake, uncovered, in hot oven about 15 minutes or until cooked through.

**SERVES 4**

Per Serving 12.9g fat; 1761kJ
**Store** Chicken can be prepared several hours ahead; keep, covered, in refrigerator. Freeze crumbed chicken for up to 2 months. Cook just before serving time.

# Beef

# Garlic mustard steak salad

**PREPARATION TIME** 15 minutes
**COOKING TIME** 10 minutes

    2  cloves garlic, crushed
1kg  piece rump steak
    2  tablespoons oil
    1  medium carrot (120g)
    1  small green cucumber (130g), seeded
    1  medium red onion (170g), sliced

### Dressing

$\frac{1}{2}$  cup (125ml) olive oil
$\frac{1}{4}$  cup (60ml) white vinegar
    1  tablespoon chopped fresh parsley
    1  tablespoon seeded mustard
    1  teaspoon caster sugar

Rub garlic over both sides of steak. Heat oil in medium frying pan, add steak, cook until browned both sides and cooked as desired. Remove steak from pan. Cut steak into strips, reserve any juices.

Meanwhile, cut carrot and cucumber into strips. Place onion in a heatproof bowl, cover with boiling water, stand 5 minutes; drain.

Combine steak, reserved juices, carrot, cucumber, onion and Dressing in large bowl.

**Dressing** Combine all ingredients in jar; shake well.

**SERVES 4**

**Per Serving** 50.7g fat; 2926kJ
**Store** Salad can be made several hours ahead; keep, covered, in refrigerator.

# Beef stroganoff

**PREPARATION TIME** 10 minutes
**COOKING TIME** 20 minutes

750g  rump steak, sliced thinly
  2  tablespoons plain flour
  1  teaspoon sweet paprika
60g  butter
  2  small onions (160g), chopped finely
  2  cloves garlic, crushed
250g  button mushrooms
  1  tablespoon lemon juice
  2  tablespoons dry red wine
  2  tablespoons tomato paste
1½  cups (375ml) sour cream
  2  tablespoons chopped fresh chives

Place steak in plastic bag with flour and paprika, shake until steak is well coated with flour mixture.

Melt butter in medium saucepan, add onion and garlic, stir constantly over medium heat for about 3 minutes or until onion is soft. Increase heat to high, add steak gradually to saucepan; stir constantly until all steak is browned all over.

Add mushrooms, juice and wine, stir until ingredients are combined. Reduce heat; cover, simmer over low heat for about 5 minutes or until steak is tender.

Stir in tomato paste and sour cream, stir constantly over heat until mixture is heated through. Serve with boiled pasta or rice if desired; sprinkle with chives before serving.

**SERVES 2**

Per Serving 116.9g fat; 6376kJ

**Store** Stroganoff can be made a day ahead without the sour cream and tomato paste. Keep, covered, in refrigerator. Stroganoff will freeze for up to 2 months without the mushrooms, sour cream and tomato paste. Add these after reheating steak mixture.

# Moroccan beef salad with couscous

**PREPARATION TIME**
15 minutes (plus standing time)

**COOKING TIME** 10 minutes

| | |
|---|---|
| 1 | cup (250ml) vegetable stock |
| 1$\frac{1}{2}$ | cups (300g) couscous |
| 500g | rump steak, in one piece |
| $\frac{1}{2}$ | cup (75g) dried apricots, sliced |
| $\frac{1}{2}$ | cup (80g) sultanas |
| 1 | medium red onion (170g), sliced thinly |
| $\frac{1}{4}$ | cup finely chopped fresh mint leaves |
| 2 | tablespoons finely chopped fresh dill |
| 1 | tablespoon pine nuts |
| 2 | teaspoons cumin seeds |
| $\frac{3}{4}$ | cup (180ml) French dressing |

Bring stock to boil in large pan; remove from heat. Add couscous to pan, cover, stand about 5 minutes or until stock is absorbed.

Meanwhile, cook beef on heated oiled grill plate (or grill or barbecue) until browned both sides and cooked as desired; slice beef thinly.

Fluff couscous with fork, add apricots, sultanas, onion and herbs; mix gently.

Place pine nuts and cumin in small dry pan; stir over low heat until seeds are just fragrant and pine nuts are toasted. Watch carefully that they don't burn. Combine seeds and nuts with dressing in small bowl. Serve beef over couscous; drizzle with dressing mixture.

**SERVES 4**

**Per Serving** 20.6g fat; 2959kJ
**Store** Best made close to serving time.

# Fillet of beef with horseradish cream

**PREPARATION TIME** 10 minutes
**COOKING TIME** 25 minutes

  2  x 750g pieces eye fillet, trimmed
  2  teaspoons cracked black peppercorns
90g  butter
  2  tablespoons plain flour
  2  cups (500ml) beef stock
  2  tablespoons brandy
200g  button mushrooms, sliced

### Horseradish Cream

  ½  cup (125ml) horseradish relish
  ½  cup (125ml) sour cream

Secure beef with string at 5cm intervals. Press peppercorns firmly onto beef. Melt butter in large baking dish, add beef, cook over high heat about 5 minutes or until browned all over. Bake in moderately hot oven about 20 minutes for rare beef, or until cooked as desired. Remove beef from dish, remove string, keep beef warm.

Pour excess drippings from dish, leaving ¼ cup in dish, stir in flour, stir over medium heat for about 5 minutes or until flour is browned. Remove from heat, gradually stir in combined stock, brandy and mushrooms, stir over high heat until sauce boils and thickens. Slice beef and serve with sauce, Horseradish Cream and vegetables of your choice.

**Horseradish cream** Combine horseradish relish and sour cream in a small bowl.

### SERVES 6

**Per Serving** 34.9g fat; 2435kJ
**Store** Beef is best cooked close to serving time. Horseradish Cream can be made 3 days ahead; keep, covered, in refrigerator.

# Garlic beef and daikon with pine nuts

**PREPARATION TIME** 10 minutes
**COOKING TIME** 15 minutes

|   |   |
|---|---|
| 1 | tablespoon vegetable oil |
| 500g | fillet steak, sliced thinly |
| 3 | cloves garlic, crushed |
| 1/2 | medium daikon (300g), sliced thinly |
| 4 | green onions, chopped |
| 2 | tablespoons chopped fresh coriander |
| 2 | tablespoons lemon juice |
| 2 | teaspoons sugar |
| 1 | teaspoon cornflour |
| 1/4 | cup (60ml) beef stock |
| 1/2 | cup (80g) pine nuts, toasted |

Heat oil in wok. Add combined beef and garlic in batches. Stir-fry until beef is tender, remove.

Add daikon to wok, stir-fry. Add beef, green onions, coriander, juice, sugar and blended cornflour and stock. Stir until mixture boils and thickens slightly. Sprinkle with pine nuts.

**SERVES 4**

**Per Serving** 25g fat; 1554kJ
**Store** Best made close to serving time.

# Herbed rissoles with mushroom sauce

**PREPARATION TIME** 10 minutes
**COOKING TIME** 30 minutes

750g minced beef
  1 medium brown onion (150g), chopped finely
  1 medium carrot (120g), grated coarsely
  1 medium red capsicum (200g), chopped finely
  2 teaspoons fresh thyme leaves
  2 cloves garlic, crushed
  2 eggs, beaten lightly
  ½ cup (75g) plain flour
30g butter
  1 tablespoon vegetable oil

## Mushroom Sauce

  ⅓ cup (50g) plain flour
  ⅓ cup (80ml) dry red wine
  2 cups (500ml) beef stock
  6 green onions, chopped finely
125g button mushrooms, sliced

Combine mince, onion, carrot, capsicum, thyme, garlic and egg in medium bowl. Mix with wooden spoon until ingredients are well combined.

Divide mixture into 8 equal portions, roll into balls, flatten slightly into rissole shapes. Place flour in shallow bowl or plate, toss rissoles in flour, shake off excess flour.

Heat butter and oil in medium frying pan over medium heat. Add rissoles, cook for about 10 minutes on each side. Turn rissoles with egg slice several times during cooking; drain on absorbent paper.

**Mushroom sauce** Measure approximately 4 tablespoons of the pan drippings into small saucepan; stir in flour, stir constantly over medium heat about 1 minute or until flour mixture browns lightly. Gradually stir in combined wine and stock; stir constantly over high heat until sauce boils and thickens. Add green onions and mushrooms to sauce, simmer for 2 minutes.

Place rissoles on serving plates, pour Sauce over rissoles and serve with the vegetables of your choice.

**MAKES 8**

Per Serving 17.2g fat; 1323kJ
**Store** Rissoles can be made a day ahead; keep, covered, in refrigerator. Freeze uncooked and unfloured rissoles for up to 2 months.

# Beef and haloumi kebabs

**PREPARATION TIME** 15 minutes
**COOKING TIME** 10 minutes

*Soak bamboo skewers in water*
*for 20 minutes to prevent burning.*

|     |     |
| --- | --- |
| 1kg | rump steak |
| 350g | haloumi cheese |
| 1 | tablespoon chopped fresh thyme leaves |
| 1/4 | cup chopped fresh mint leaves |
| 2 | cloves garlic, crushed |
| 1/4 | cup (60ml) lemon juice |
| 1/3 | cup (80ml) olive oil |
| 1 | tablespoon olive oil, extra |

Cut steak and haloumi into 2cm cubes, then halve cheese cubes. Thread steak and haloumi alternately on skewers. Combine thyme, mint, garlic, juice and oil in jug; brush over kebabs.

Heat extra oil in large pan; cook kebabs, in batches, brushing occasionally with herb and oil mixture, until browned all over and cooked as desired.

**SERVES 4**

**Per Serving** 50.6g fat; 3150kJ
**Store** Kebabs can be marinated in herb and oil mixture for several hours or overnight. Cook just before serving time.

# Water spinach and beef soup

**PREPARATION TIME**
20 minutes (plus marinating time)

**COOKING TIME** 10 minutes

*Chinese water spinach is a mild, versatile vegetable with crunchy white stalks and tender, dark green leaves. It resembles a bunch of spinach (which can be substituted) but has longer, more flexible leaves.*

500g beef fillet, sliced thinly
  2 cloves garlic, crushed
  3 green onions, sliced thinly
  2 teaspoons fish sauce
  1 teaspoon sugar
  1 red Thai chilli, seeded, chopped finely
  2 teaspoons grated fresh galangal
500g Chinese water spinach
1.5 litres (6 cups) water
  2 tablespoons lemon juice
1/4 cup loosely packed torn fresh Vietnamese mint leaves

Place beef, garlic, onion, sauce, sugar, chilli and galangal in large bowl; toss to combine. Cover; refrigerate 10 minutes.

Trim spinach stems; crush stems with meat mallet or rolling pin. Chop leaves coarsely.

Bring the water to boil in large saucepan, add spinach and beef mixture. Simmer, uncovered, 2 minutes.

Remove soup from heat; stir in remaining ingredients.

**SERVES 6**

**Per Serving** 4.5g fat; 555kJ
**Store** This soup will be at its most flavoursome if you marinate the beef overnight. Keep, covered, in refrigerator. Make the soup as close to serving time as possible.

# Stir-fried Mexican beef

**PREPARATION TIME** 20 minutes
**COOKING TIME** 15 minutes

*You can use rib eye (Scotch fillet),
rump, sirloin or topside in this
recipe if you prefer.*

750g  eye fillet, sliced thinly
 35g  packet taco seasoning
   1  tablespoon peanut oil
   1  large red onion (300g), sliced thinly
   1  medium red capsicum (200g),
      sliced thinly
   1  medium yellow capsicum (200g),
      sliced thinly
   4  small tomatoes (520g), seeded, sliced
   2  tablespoons fresh coriander leaves

Combine beef and seasoning in medium
bowl. Heat half the oil in wok or large pan;
stir-fry beef mixture and onion, in batches,
until well browned.

Heat remaining oil in wok, stir-fry capsicums
until just tender.

Return beef mixture to wok with tomato
and coriander; stir-fry until hot.

**SERVES 4**

**Per Serving** 14.3g fat; 1514kJ
**Store** Beef can be marinated in taco seasoning
several hours or overnight; keep, covered,
in refrigerator.

*Lamb*

# Lamb with tomatoes, fetta and olives

**PREPARATION TIME** 20 minutes
**COOKING TIME** 15 minutes

250g green beans, halved
  2 tablespoons olive oil
500g lamb fillets, sliced thinly
  2 cloves garlic, crushed
  1 teaspoon cracked black peppercorns
  1 medium brown onion (150g), quartered
250g cherry tomatoes
  1 cup (160g) black olives
200g fetta cheese, cubed
  1 teaspoon grated lemon rind
  2 tablespoons lemon juice
  1 tablespoon chopped fresh oregano

Add beans to pan of boiling water, drain; rinse under cold water, drain.

Heat half the oil in wok. Add combined lamb, garlic and peppercorns, in batches, stir-fry until lamb is tender, remove.

Heat remaining oil in wok. Add beans and onion, stir-fry. Add lamb and remaining ingredients, stir-fry until hot.

**SERVES 4**

**Per Serving** 32.5g fat; 2094kJ
**Store** Lamb, half the oil, garlic, peppercorns, rind, juice and oregano can be marinated several hours or overnight. Keep, covered, in refrigerator.

# Lamb, fetta and parsley triangles

PREPARATION TIME 20 minutes
COOKING TIME 15 minutes

700g  minced lamb
250g  fetta cheese, crumbled
  1/3  cup chopped fresh parsley
   1  tablespoon sumac
   1  tablespoon ground cumin
   2  cloves garlic, crushed
   2  eggs, beaten
   1  teaspoon cracked black pepper
  16  sheets fillo pastry
125g  butter, melted

Using your hands, combine lamb, cheese, parsley, sumac, cumin, garlic, eggs and pepper in large bowl.

To prevent fillo drying out, cover with damp tea-towel until ready to use. Brush 1 sheet of fillo with some of the butter; fold in half, brush with more butter. Place 1/3 cup lamb mixture in one corner, 1cm in from edge, flatten slightly. Fold opposite corner of fillo diagonally across the filling to form a large triangle. Continue folding to end of fillo, retaining triangular shape. Repeat with remaining fillo, butter and lamb mixture.

Brush triangles with melted butter; bake on lightly oiled oven trays in moderately hot oven about 15 minutes or until browned lightly and cooked through.

### MAKES 16

Per Triangle 15.6g fat; 1002kJ
Store Triangles can be made several hours ahead and reheated at serving time. Keep, covered, in refrigerator.

# Grilled lamb pizza with rosemary vinaigrette

**PREPARATION TIME** 20 minutes
**COOKING TIME** 20 minutes

*We used large (25cm diameter)
packaged pizza bases for this recipe.*

- 8 lamb schnitzels
- 2 tablespoons Dijon mustard
- 4 cloves garlic, crushed
- 1 tablespoon finely chopped fresh rosemary
- 2 tablespoons olive oil
- 250g button mushrooms, halved
- 2 x 355g pizza bases
- 1/2 cup (125ml) bottled tomato pasta sauce
- 3 cups (375g) coarsely grated pizza cheese
- 1/2 cup (30g) sun-dried tomatoes in oil, drained
- 200g baby spinach leaves
- 1/4 cup (20g) flaked parmesan cheese

Rosemary Vinaigrette

- 2 tablespoons white wine vinegar
- 1 tablespoon seeded mustard
- 1/3 cup (25g) finely grated parmesan cheese
- 2 teaspoons finely chopped fresh rosemary
- 2 cloves garlic, crushed
- 1/2 cup (125ml) olive oil

Place lamb between sheets of plastic wrap; pound until an even thickness. Coat lamb with combined mustard, garlic, rosemary and oil in shallow dish.

Cook mushrooms in small heated oiled pan, stirring, about 5 minutes or until browned lightly and tender.

Place pizza bases on oiled oven trays; spread with pasta sauce; sprinkle with pizza cheese, mushrooms and halved tomatoes. Bake, uncovered, in hot oven about 15 minutes or until pizzas are just browned and bases crisp.

Meanwhile, cook lamb on heated oiled grill plate (or grill or barbecue) until browned both sides and cooked through.

Gently toss spinach with rosemary vinaigrette in large bowl. Place lamb and spinach on pizzas; sprinkle with parmesan.

**Rosemary vinaigrette** Combine all ingredients in jar; shake well.

SERVES 4

Per serving 76.5g fat; 6080kJ
Store Lamb can be marinated several hours or overnight; keep, covered, in refrigerator. Lamb and marinade can be frozen for up to 2 months.

# Pork and Veal

# Hoisin pork with green beans

**PREPARATION TIME** 15 minutes
**COOKING TIME** 15 minutes

| | |
|---|---|
| 1 | tablespoon peanut oil |
| 500g | pork fillets, sliced thinly |
| 1 | birdseye chilli, chopped finely |
| 1 | teaspoon grated fresh ginger |
| 1 | clove garlic, crushed |
| 1 | teaspoon sesame oil |
| 2 | tablespoons hoisin sauce |
| 1 | small leek (200g), chopped |
| 2 | teaspoons fish sauce |
| 250g | green beans, sliced |

Heat half the peanut oil in wok. Add combined pork, chilli, ginger, garlic, sesame oil and hoisin sauce, in batches; stir-fry until pork is tender, remove.

Heat remaining peanut oil in wok, add leek and stir-fry. Add pork and fish sauce, stir until heated through.

Meanwhile, bring small saucepan of water to boil; add beans. Return to boil for 1 minute; drain. Serve pork mixture over beans.

**SERVES 4**

Per Serving 9.4g fat; 972kJ
**Store** Pork, chilli, ginger, garlic, sesame oil and hoisin sauce can be marinated for several hours or overnight; keep, covered, in refrigerator.

# Veal parmigiana

**PREPARATION TIME** 20 minutes
**COOKING TIME** 20 minutes

- 1  medium eggplant (300g)
- 8  veal leg steaks (800g)
     plain flour
- 2  tablespoons olive oil
- 1  clove garlic, crushed
- 4  large tomatoes (1kg), chopped
- ¼  cup shredded fresh basil leaves
- 1  teaspoon sugar
- 1  cup (100g) grated mozzarella cheese
- 1  tablespoon grated parmesan cheese

Cut eggplant lengthways into 8 slices, make shallow cuts in criss-cross pattern on one side of each slice. Brush both sides with a little of the oil; grill until browned.

Meanwhile, place steaks between sheets of plastic wrap; pound with meat mallet until an even thickness. Toss in flour; shake off excess. Heat half the remaining oil in large pan; cook steaks, in batches, until browned both sides and cooked as desired. Remove from pan; cover to keep warm.

Heat remaining oil in same pan, add garlic; cook until soft. Add tomatoes, basil and sugar, simmer, uncovered, about 15 minutes or until tomatoes are soft and sauce thickens.

Top each steak with slice of eggplant, spoon sauce over; sprinkle with cheeses. Grill until cheeses have melted.

**SERVES 4**

Per Serving 20.5g fat; 1848kJ
Store Can be prepared 3 hours ahead; keep, covered, in refrigerator.

# Pork and macadamia stir-fried salad

**PREPARATION TIME** 15 minutes
**COOKING TIME** 20 minutes

> 1 tablespoon light olive oil
> 1 small kumara (250g), sliced thinly
> ¼ cup (35g) macadamias
> 500g pork fillets, sliced thinly
> 2 tablespoons teriyaki sauce
> 1 teaspoon grated orange rind
> 1 clove garlic, crushed
> 1 teaspoon cracked black peppercorns
> 200g Swiss brown mushrooms, halved
> 4 green onions, chopped
> 2 tablespoons cider vinegar
> ⅓ cup (80ml) light olive oil, extra
> ¼ teaspoon sugar
> 120g rocket
> ¼ cup small fresh basil leaves

Heat half the oil in wok. Add kumara, stir-fry until just tender, remove. Add nuts to wok, stir-fry until lightly browned, remove.

Heat remaining oil in wok, add combined pork, sauce, rind, garlic and peppercorns in batches, stir-fry until pork is tender, remove.

Add mushrooms and green onions to wok, stir-fry until mushrooms have softened slightly.

Return kumara and pork mixture to wok with vinegar, extra oil and sugar, stir until hot. Add rocket and basil. Serve sprinkled with nuts.

**SERVES 4**

Per Serving 32.8g fat; 1976kJ
Store Pork, sauce, rind, garlic and peppercorns can be marinated several hours or overnight; keep, covered, in refrigerator.

# Pork with mushrooms, ginger and bok choy

**PREPARATION TIME**
10 minutes (plus standing time)
**COOKING TIME** 10 minutes

| | |
|---|---|
| 8 | dried shiitake mushrooms |
| 1 | tablespoon peanut oil |
| 3 | teaspoons grated fresh ginger |
| 450g | pork fillets, sliced thinly |
| 150g | oyster mushrooms |
| 150g | button mushrooms, halved |
| 1 | tablespoon hoisin sauce |
| 1 | teaspoon cornflour |
| ½ | cup (125ml) chicken stock |
| 250g | bok choy, chopped roughly |

Place mushrooms in small heatproof bowl, cover with boiling water, stand 20 minutes, drain. Discard stems, slice caps finely.

Heat oil in wok. Add ginger, stir-fry until fragrant. Add pork in batches, stir-fry until tender, remove. Add all mushrooms to wok, stir-fry until hot.

Add pork, sauce and blended cornflour and stock, stir until sauce boils and thickens slightly. Add bok choy, stir-fry until just wilted.

**SERVES 4**

Per Serving 7.9g fat; 889kJ
Store Best made close to serving time.

# Veal marsala

**PREPARATION TIME** 10 minutes
**COOKING TIME** 15 minutes

- 8 veal leg schnitzels (800g)
  plain flour
- 2 tablespoons vegetable oil
- 20g butter
- 1/3 cup (80ml) marsala
- 3/4 cup (180ml) cream
- 1/2 teaspoon cracked black peppercorns
- 2 tablespoons chopped fresh chives

Toss schnitzels in flour; shake off excess. Heat oil and butter in large frying pan; cook schnitzels, in batches, until browned both sides and cooked as desired. Remove schnitzels from pan, cover to keep warm.

Drain fat from pan. Add remaining ingredients to pan; simmer, stirring, until sauce thickens slightly. Return schnitzels and any juices to pan, coat with sauce; serve immediately with vegetables of your choice.

**SERVES 4**

**Per Serving** 37.8g fat; 2380kJ
**Store** Best made close to serving time.

# Ginger veal stir-fry

**PREPARATION TIME** 10 minutes
**COOKING TIME** 15 minutes

- 1/4 cup (60ml) peanut oil
- 4 veal steaks (500g), sliced
- 2 medium zucchini (240g), sliced
- 100g snow peas
- 100g green beans
- 1 medium red capsicum (200g), chopped
- 2/3 cup (110g) pitted prunes
- 1/4 cup (60ml) dry sherry
- 1 teaspoon dark soy sauce
- 2 teaspoons lime juice
- 1/2 teaspoon ground ginger
- 1 tablespoon sugar
- 1 1/2 tablespoons cornflour
- 1/4 cup (60ml) water

Heat 2 tablespoons oil in large wok, add veal, stir-fry until browned all over; remove. Add remaining oil to same wok; add vegetables and prunes, stir-fry until vegetables are just tender. Stir in sherry, sauce, juice, ginger, sugar and blended cornflour and water, stir until mixture boils and thickens. Return veal to pan, stir until heated through. Serve with rice or noodles, if desired.

**SERVES 4**

**Per Serving** 17.2g fat; 1617kJ
**Store** Best made close to serving time.

# Pork and veal parcels with apricot sauce

**PREPARATION TIME** 15 minutes
**COOKING TIME** 30 minutes

425g  can apricot halves in syrup, drained
370g  minced pork and veal
    1  small brown onion (80g), chopped
    1  clove garlic, crushed
    1  teaspoon grated fresh ginger
    2  tablespoons chopped fresh coriander
    2  tablespoons stale breadcrumbs
       plain flour
    2  tablespoons olive oil
  16  sheets fillo pastry
100g  butter, melted
  $^{1}/_{2}$  cup (35g) stale breadcrumbs, extra

### Apricot Sauce

  1  teaspoon ground cumin
  2  tablespoons mango chutney
$^{1}/_{3}$  cup (80ml) apricot nectar

Finely chop 10 apricot halves. Reserve remaining apricots for sauce.

Combine chopped apricots, mince, onion, garlic, ginger, coriander and breadcrumbs in bowl. Using floured hands, shape mixture into 8 patties. Cook patties in hot oil until browned; drain on absorbent paper.

To prevent fillo from drying out, cover with a damp tea-towel until ready to use. Layer 4 sheets of fillo together, brushing each with butter and sprinkling with extra breadcrumbs. Cut fillo in half, place 1 patty on each half, fold into parcels, brush with remaining butter. Place on greased oven tray; continue with remaining fillo and patties. Bake, uncovered, in moderate oven about 25 minutes or until browned. Serve parcels with Apricot Sauce.

**Apricot sauce** Blend or process reserved apricots, cumin, chutney and nectar until mixture is smooth.

### SERVES 4

**Per Serving** 38.5g fat; 3039kJ
**Store** Recipe can be prepared a day ahead; keep, covered, in refrigerator.

# Veal pizzaiola

**PREPARATION TIME** 10 minutes
**COOKING TIME** 20 minutes

2 teaspoons olive oil
1 clove garlic, crushed
2 tablespoons dry white wine
1 tablespoon chopped fresh oregano
$1/2$ cup (125ml) beef stock
3 cups (750ml) bottled chunky tomato pasta sauce
$2/3$ cup (80g) small black olives
4 veal steaks (500g)

Heat non-stick saucepan with half the oil. Add garlic, wine and oregano; simmer, uncovered, until reduced by half. Add stock and sauce; simmer, uncovered, about 10 minutes or until sauce thickens slightly. Stir in olives.

Heat remaining oil in large non-stick saucepan; cook veal, until browned both sides and cooked as desired. Serve veal with sauce and the vegetables of your choice.

**SERVES 4**

Per Serving 7g fat; 1250kJ
Store Sauce can be made a day ahead; keep, covered, in refrigerator. Sauce can be frozen for up to 3 months.

# Gingered pork with vegetables

**PREPARATION TIME** 10 minutes
**COOKING TIME** 15 minutes

700g pork fillets, sliced thinly
  2 tablespoons grated fresh ginger
  ¼ cup chopped fresh coriander leaves
  2 tablespoons rice vinegar
  2 tablespoons peanut oil
125g fresh baby corn, halved lengthways
  1 medium red capsicum (200g),
    sliced thinly
100g snow peas, halved
  2 tablespoons light soy sauce
250g spinach, trimmed
  3 cups bean sprouts (240g)
  ½ cup fresh coriander leaves, extra

Combine pork, ginger, coriander and vinegar in medium bowl.

Heat half of the oil in wok; stir-fry pork mixture, in batches, until pork is browned and cooked through; remove.

Heat remaining oil in same wok; stir-fry corn, capsicum and peas until just tender, remove from wok. Return pork to wok with sauce; stir-fry until heated through. Gently toss cooked vegetables with pork, spinach, sprouts and extra coriander until spinach just wilts.

**SERVES 4**

Per Serving 13.8g fat; 1437kJ
**Store** Best made close to serving time.

# Veal cutlets with roasted tomatoes and spinach salad

**PREPARATION TIME** 15 minutes
**COOKING TIME** 35 minutes

|   |   |
|---|---|
| 9 | small egg tomatoes (540g), halved |
|   | ground black pepper |
| ¼ | cup (60ml) olive oil |
| 120g | baby beans |
| 6 | veal cutlets (750g) |
| ¼ | cup small basil leaves |
| 100g | baby spinach leaves |
| 1 | small red onion (100g), sliced thinly |
| 60g | butter |

**Garlic Dressing**

|   |   |
|---|---|
| ½ | cup (125ml) olive oil |
| 2 | tablespoons balsamic vinegar |
| 3 | cloves garlic, crushed |
| 1 | teaspoon English mustard |

Place tomatoes in oiled baking dish; drizzle with 1 tablespoon of the oil. Cook in hot oven for 30 minutes or until soft.

Meanwhile place beans in heatproof bowl, cover with boiling water; stand 2 minutes, drain. Cool under cold water. Combine beans, basil, spinach and onion in large bowl.

Heat butter and remaining oil in large frying pan and cook cutlets until browned on both sides and cooked as desired.

Toss spinach salad with Garlic Dressing. Serve cutlets with salad and tomatoes.

**Garlic Dressing** Combine all ingredients in jar; shake well.

### SERVES 6

**Per Serving** 21.9g fat; 1282kJ
**Store** Best made just before serving.
Garlic Dressing can be made a day ahead; store, covered, in refrigerator.

# Barbecued pork and vegetable soup

**PREPARATION TIME** 10 minutes
**COOKING TIME** 10 minutes

 2 teaspoons peanut oil
 1 clove garlic, crushed
 1 birdseye chilli, chopped finely
 2 teaspoons grated fresh ginger
 1.5 litres (6 cups) chicken stock
 5 green onions, chopped
 1 medium carrot (120g), sliced thinly
 1/2 x 425g can straw mushrooms, drained, halved
 100g Chinese broccoli, shredded
 1/2 x 425g can baby corn, drained, halved
 250g Chinese barbecued pork, sliced

Heat oil in large pan, add garlic, chilli and ginger, cook, stirring, 1 minute. Add stock, green onions and carrot, bring to boil, simmer, uncovered, about 5 minutes or until carrot is tender.

Add mushrooms, broccoli, corn and pork, simmer, uncovered, a few minutes or until heated through.

**SERVES 6**

Per Serving 9.2g fat; 709kJ
Store Best made close to serving time.

# Wraps on the run

**Chicken and pickled cucumber pitta**

*All wraps can be made in 20 minutes or less and serve 4.*

## Smoked salmon and roasted vegetable lavash

        2  large red capsicums (700g)
        6  baby eggplants (360g)
        4  medium zucchini (480g)
        4  lavash breads
    250g  rocket leaves
    200g  sliced smoked salmon
        1  lemon

Quarter capsicums, remove and discard seeds and membranes. Roast under grill or in very hot oven, skin-side up, until skin blisters and blackens. Cover capsicum pieces with plastic or paper for 5 minutes, peel away skin; slice capsicum thinly.

Meanwhile, slice eggplants and zucchini lengthways. Place in single layer on oiled oven trays. Cook under hot grill or in hot oven until lightly browned both sides.

Roll each piece of bread into a cone shape; fill with eggplant, rocket, zucchini, capsicum and salmon. Sprinkle with 1 teaspoon shredded lemon rind and drizzle with 2 teaspoons lemon juice.

**Per Serving** 5g fat; 1402kJ

## Chicken and pickled cucumber pitta

    1  single chicken breast fillet (170g)
    1  medium green cucumber (170g)
    1  tablespoon cider vinegar
    2  teaspoons sugar
    1  birdseye chilli, seeded, chopped finely
    1  teaspoon soy sauce
    1  small butter lettuce
    4  pocket pitta breads

Cook chicken on heated oiled grill plate (or grill or barbecue) until browned both sides and cooked through; cool. Slice chicken thinly.

Meanwhile, slice cucumber into long, thin strips with a vegetable peeler. Combine cucumber, vinegar, sugar, chilli and sauce in medium bowl; stand 10 minutes.

Serve chicken, pickled cucumber and lettuce in pitta.

**Per Serving** 4.3g fat; 1276kJ

# Eggplant rolls

¼ cup (60ml) olive oil
1 clove garlic, crushed
1 large eggplant (about 500g), sliced
4 slices wholemeal Lebanese bread
⅓ cup (80ml) hummus
1 medium brown onion (150g), sliced
2 large tomatoes (about 500g), sliced
⅓ cup chopped fresh flat-leafed parsley
1 tablespoon chopped fresh mint
150g fetta cheese, crumbled

Combine oil and garlic in bowl; reserve 2 teaspoons of the oil mixture. Brush eggplant with remaining oil mixture, cook on a ridged grill pan until lightly browned.

Spread each slice of bread with hummus, top with some eggplant, onion, tomato, herbs and cheese. Roll bread around filling, secure with skewers, brush with reserved oil mixture.

Place rolls on oven tray, bake, uncovered, in moderately hot oven about 10 minutes or until crisp and heated through.

**Per Serving** 28.6g fat; 2493kJ

**Smoked salmon and vegetable lavash, eggplant rolls (back)**

# Tandoori lamb naan

250g lamb fillets
1 tablespoon tandoori paste
¾ cup (180ml) low-fat yogurt
4 naan breads
2 tablespoons chopped fresh mint leaves
1 tablespoon lime juice
100g curly endive
1 Lebanese cucumber (130g), seeded, sliced finely

Combine lamb, paste and ¼ cup (60ml) of the yogurt in medium bowl; cover, refrigerate 10 minutes.

Cook lamb on heated oiled grill plate (or grill or barbecue) until browned all over and cooked as desired; slice lamb.

Meanwhile, heat naan according to packet directions.

Blend or process remaining yogurt, mint and juice until smooth.

Place lamb, endive, cucumber and yogurt mixture in centre of naan; roll up to enclose filling.

**Per Serving** 9.5g fat; 1164kJ

# Pasta

# Veal and fettuccine with mustard cream sauce

**PREPARATION TIME** 10 minutes
**COOKING TIME** 25 minutes

| | |
|---:|:---|
| 1/4 | cup (60ml) olive oil |
| 1 | medium brown onion (150g), sliced |
| 750g | veal shank |
| | plain flour |
| 1/2 | cup (125ml) buttermilk |
| 3/4 | cup (180ml) cream |
| 1/2 | cup (125ml) dry white wine |
| 2 | tablespoons French mustard |
| 500g | fresh plain and spinach fettuccine |

Heat 1 tablespoon of the oil in pan, add onion, cook, stirring, until soft; remove from pan.

Remove meat from shank, cut meat into strips. Toss meat in flour, shake away excess flour. Heat remaining oil in pan, add meat, cook, stirring, until well browned and tender; remove from pan, combine with onion in bowl.

Boil any juices remaining in pan on high heat for about 1 minute or until reduced to about 1 tablespoon. Add buttermilk to pan, stir over heat until mixture thickens slightly. Stir in cream, wine and mustard, stir until mixture boils; simmer, uncovered, until slightly thickened.

Meanwhile, add pasta to large pan of boiling water, boil, uncovered, until just tender, drain; keep warm.

Add veal and onion to mustard sauce, stir until heated through, serve over pasta.

**SERVES 4**

**Per Serving** 37.1g fat; 3748kJ
**Store** Best made close to serving time.

# Fettuccine carbonara

**PREPARATION TIME** 10 minutes
**COOKING TIME** 15 minutes

250g dried fettuccine
 30g softened butter
  4 rashers bacon or pancetta
    (Italian cured bacon)
 1/3 cup (80ml) cream
    pinch sweet paprika
  1 egg
  1 egg yolk, extra
 60g grated parmesan cheese
    pepper

Add pasta to large pan of boiling salted water; boil, uncovered, until just tender; drain. Return pasta to pan with butter, toss over low heat until combined.

Meanwhile, remove rind from bacon, cut bacon into thin strips. Place bacon in large frying pan over low heat, cook gently until crisp. Drain off fat from pan, leaving approximately 2 tablespoons.

Add cream and paprika to pan, stir until combined. Place egg, egg yolk and half the cheese in bowl, beat until combined.

Add cream mixture, egg mixture and bacon to pasta, toss until combined. Season with pepper. Sprinkle with remaining grated parmesan cheese.

**SERVES 4**

Per Serving 24.4g fat; 2004kJ
Store Best made close to serving time.

# Farfalle with broccoli and parmesan

**PREPARATION TIME** 20 minutes
**COOKING TIME** 10 minutes

500g farfalle pasta
1½ cups (375ml) buttermilk
1 clove garlic, crushed
1 tablespoon Dijon mustard
¼ cup (60ml) olive oil
425g broccoli, chopped
½ cup (40g) flaked almonds, toasted
½ cup (40g) grated fresh parmesan cheese
6 green onions, sliced finely
80g snow pea sprouts

Cook pasta in large saucepan of boiling water, uncovered, until just tender; drain.

Meanwhile, place buttermilk, garlic, mustard and oil in small bowl; whisk until combined.

Boil, steam or microwave broccoli until tender.

Combine hot pasta, buttermilk mixture, broccoli, nuts, cheese and onion. Stir through and serve with sprouts.

**SERVES 4**

Per Serving 26.3g fat; 3134kJ
Store Best made close to serving time.

# Mediterranean tortellini

Fork and bowl: *Empire Homewares, Paddington*

**PREPARATION TIME** 10 minutes
**COOKING TIME** 15 minutes

  2  **medium red capsicums (400g)**
  1  **tablespoon olive oil**
  2  **cloves garlic, crushed**
  1  **birdseye chilli, seeded, sliced**
  4  **large egg tomatoes (360g), chopped**
  6  **artichoke hearts in oil, quartered**
  ½  **cup (80g) black olives, stoned, sliced**
  1  **tablespoon oregano leaves**
750g  **cheese and spinach tortellini**

Quarter capsicum, remove seeds and membranes. Grill capsicum, skin side up, until skin blisters and blackens. Cover capsicum pieces with plastic or paper for 5 minutes. Peel away skin, slice capsicums thickly.

Heat oil in large pan add garlic and chilli, cook, stirring, until fragrant. Add capsicum, tomatoes and artichokes, cook, stirring until hot. Stir in olives and oregano.

Meanwhile, cook tortellini in large pan of boiling salted water, uncovered, until just tender; drain. Serve sauce over tortellini.

**SERVES 6**

**Per Serving** 15.3g fat; 1211kJ
**Store** Sauce can be made a day ahead; store, covered, in refrigerator.

# Linguine with smoked trout and horseradish

**PREPARATION TIME** 10 minutes
**COOKING TIME** 15 minutes

375g  dried linguine
500g  spinach, trimmed, shredded
   1 cup (125g) grated cheddar cheese

**Trout Sauce**

   1  tablespoon olive oil
   6  green onions, sliced
   2  cloves garlic, crushed
   1  tablespoon chopped fresh thyme
   2  small smoked rainbow trout (600g), skinned, boned, flaked
$^3/_4$  cup (180ml) sour cream
$^1/_2$  cup (125ml) water
   2  tablespoons horseradish relish

Cook pasta in large pan boiling water until tender; drain. Stir spinach into pasta. Divide pasta among 6 heatproof serving dishes, top with Trout Sauce; sprinkle with cheese. Cook under hot grill until cheese is melted and golden.

**Trout sauce** Heat oil in large pan, add onions, garlic and thyme; cook until fragrant. Stir remaining ingredients into pan; stir over medium heat until heated through.

**SERVES 6**

**Per Serving** 25.9g fat; 2199kJ
**Store** Best made close to serving time.

# Chicken, lentil and spinach pasta

**PREPARATION TIME** 10 minutes
**COOKING TIME** 20 minutes

|       |                                    |
|------:|------------------------------------|
|     2 | teaspoons vegetable oil            |
|     1 | small brown onion (80g), chopped finely |
|     2 | cloves garlic, crushed             |
|  150g | minced chicken                     |
|  1/2  | cup (100g) red lentils             |
| 2³/4  | cups (680ml) chicken stock         |
|     2 | tablespoons tomato paste           |
|  250g | baby spinach leaves                |
|  375g | shell pasta                        |

Heat oil in medium pan; cook onion and garlic, stirring, until onion softens. Add chicken; cook, stirring, until chicken has changed in colour. Stir in lentils, stock and paste; simmer, uncovered, 10 minutes or until lentils are tender and sauce thickened. Add spinach; stir until spinach is just wilted.

Meanwhile, cook pasta in large pan of boiling water, uncovered, until just tender; drain.

Combine pasta and chicken mixture in large serving bowl.

**SERVES 4**

**Per Serving** 7.8g fat; 2066kJ
**Store** Best made close to serving time.

# Veal pasta salad with lime mustard dressing

**PREPARATION TIME** 10 minutes
**COOKING TIME** 20 minutes

250g dried tagliatelle
750g veal rump steak
200g fetta cheese, chopped
  ½ cup (75g) drained sun-dried
     tomatoes, sliced
  ¼ cup (40g) pine nuts, toasted
100g mixed baby lettuce leaves
  ½ cup (60g) seeded black olives

Lime Mustard Dressing

⅓ cup (80ml) olive oil
3 teaspoons seeded mustard
1 teaspoon sugar
2 tablespoons lime juice

Cook pasta in large pan of boiling water, uncovered, until just tender; drain. Rinse under cold water; drain.

Cook steak in heated oiled grill pan (or grill or barbecue) until browned both sides and cooked as desired. Remove steak from pan, cover; stand for 5 minutes. Slice steak thinly. Combine all ingredients in large bowl with Lime Mustard Dressing.

**Lime mustard dressing** Combine all ingredients in jar; shake well.

SERVES 4

Per Serving 43.9g fat; 3586kJ
Store Best made close to serving time.

# Fettuccine with Italian sausage and olives

**PREPARATION TIME** 10 minutes
**COOKING TIME** 25 minutes

| | |
|---|---|
| 500g | fresh fettuccine |
| 500g | Italian-style pork sausages |
| 2 | tablespoons olive oil |
| 150g | button mushrooms, sliced |
| 2 | cloves garlic, crushed |
| 2/3 | cup (100g) large green olives, seeded, sliced |
| 1 | teaspoon grated lemon rind |
| 1 | tablespoon lemon juice |
| 2 | tablespoons chopped fresh parsley |
| 300ml | cream |

Add pasta to large pan of boiling water, boil, uncovered, until just tender; drain. Cook sausages in dry frying pan over medium heat, turning regularly, for 10 minutes or until browned and cooked through; drain on absorbent paper. Cut sausages into 1cm slices.

Heat oil in same pan, add mushrooms and garlic, cook, stirring, 2 minutes or until mushrooms are soft. Stir in sausages, olives, rind, juice, parsley and cream; simmer, stirring occasionally, 10 minutes or until reduced by one-third. Stir in pasta, cook, stirring, 3 minutes or until pasta is heated through.

**SERVES 4**

**Per Serving** 70.4g fat; 3712kJ
**Store** Sausages can be cooked a day ahead.

# Spaghetti with smoked salmon

**PREPARATION TIME** 15 minutes
**COOKING TIME** 15 minutes

500g  spaghetti
400g  sliced smoked salmon
    2  tablespoons olive oil
    1  medium brown onion, chopped
500g  (24 spears) fresh asparagus, halved
    1  tablespoon brandy
    2  teaspoons white mustard seeds
600ml  cream
    2  tablespoons shredded fresh basil

Cook pasta in large pan of boiling water, uncovered, until just tender; drain.

Cut salmon into 2cm strips.

Heat oil in pan; cook onion, stirring, until soft. Add salmon, asparagus, brandy, seeds and cream. Bring to boil, simmer, uncovered, until slightly thickened; stir in basil.

Stir sauce through pasta.

**SERVES 4**

Per Serving 80.3g fat; 53579kJ
Store Best made just before serving time.

# Peppered chicken and pasta salad

PREPARATION TIME 20 minutes
COOKING TIME 15 minutes

100g penne
- 1 cup (150g) chopped cooked chicken
- 1 medium red onion (170g), sliced thinly
- 1 medium apple (150g), chopped
- 2 trimmed celery sticks (150g), chopped

## Dressing

- 1 tablespoon drained canned peppercorns, chopped
- 1/3 cup (80ml) cream
- 1/4 cup (60ml) mayonnaise
- 1/2 teaspoon grated lemon rind
- 1 tablespoon lemon juice
- 1/4 teaspoon sugar

Cook pasta in large saucepan of boiling water, uncovered, until just tender; drain. Rinse pasta under cold water; drain.

Combine pasta, chicken, onion, apple and celery in bowl. Just before serving, drizzle salad with Dressing.

**Dressing** Combine all ingredients in bowl.

SERVES 4

**Per Serving** 18.2g fat; 1408kJ
**Store** Salad and dressing can be made a day ahead; keep, covered, in refrigerator.

# Roman tomato soup

**PREPARATION TIME** 10 minutes
**COOKING TIME** 15 minutes

1 tablespoon olive oil
2 cloves garlic, crushed
1 medium onion (150g), chopped finely
445g can condensed tomato soup
400g can tomatoes, undrained, crushed
3 cups (750ml) water
2 cups (210g) small fusilli (spiral pasta)
1 tablespoon finely chopped fresh
    basil leaves
2 bacon rashers, chopped finely

Heat oil in large pan; cook garlic and onion, stirring, until onion is soft. Add undiluted soup, tomatoes, water and pasta. Bring to boil; simmer, uncovered, about 10 minutes or until pasta is just tender. Stir in basil.

Meanwhile, cook bacon in medium heated oiled frying pan until browned and crisp; drain on absorbent paper. Ladle soup into serving bowls; sprinkle with bacon.

**SERVES 4**

**Per Serving** 6.1g fat; 1295kJ
**Store** Soup can be made 2 days ahead; keep, covered, in refrigerator. Soup can be frozen for up to 2 months.

# Spaghetti with chicken and red pesto

**PREPARATION TIME** 10 minutes
**COOKING TIME** 20 minutes

*We used sun-dried capsicum pesto for this recipe, but any bottled 'red' pesto, such as tomato, could be used.*

 4 **single chicken breast fillets (700g)**
 $1/4$ **cup (75g) bottled red pesto**
375g **spaghetti**
 1 **cup (70g) stale breadcrumbs**
 $1/3$ **cup finely chopped fresh chives**
 2 **teaspoons seeded mustard**
 $1/2$ **cup (125ml) chicken stock**

Coat chicken with half the pesto. Cook chicken in grill pan (or grill or barbecue) until browned both sides and cooked through; cover to keep warm.

Meanwhile, cook spaghetti in large pan of boiling water, uncovered, until just tender; drain. Rinse under cold water; drain.

Heat oiled large pan; cook breadcrumbs, stirring, until browned. Stir in spaghetti with remaining pesto, chives, mustard and stock; cook, stirring, until hot.

Serve spaghetti with sliced chicken, and tomato wedges, if desired.

**SERVES 4**

Per Serving 15.7g fat; 2805kJ
**Store** Best made close to serving time.

# *Mushroom trio with ravioli*

Waffle teatowel: *Plane Tree Farm, Double Bay*

**PREPARATION TIME** 10 minutes
**COOKING TIME** 15 minutes

750g fresh beef ravioli
   1 teaspoon olive oil
   2 cloves garlic, crushed
   2 teaspoons grated fresh ginger
   2 coriander roots, chopped
   1 birdseye chilli, seeded, chopped
250g button mushrooms, quartered
250g Swiss brown mushrooms, halved
   1 cup (250ml) evaporated skim milk
200g shiitake mushrooms, quartered
   ¼ cup fresh coriander leaves

Cook ravioli in large pan of boiling water, uncovered, until tender.

Meanwhile, heat oil in large pan; cook garlic, ginger, coriander roots and chilli until fragrant. Add button mushrooms and Swiss brown mushrooms to pan; cook, stirring, for 2 minutes. Stir in milk. Bring to boil, stirring occasionally, until milk is slightly thickened. Stir in shiitake mushrooms; cook, stirring, until hot.

Serve mushroom mixture over ravioli; sprinkle with coriander leaves.

**SERVES 4**

Per Serving 9.2g fat; 1583kJ
Store Sauce best made close to serving time.

# Angel-hair pasta with chilli

**PREPARATION TIME** 10 minutes
**COOKING TIME** 15 minutes

*We used fresh angel-hair pasta here, but any fine pasta, such as vermicelli or spaghettini, can be substituted.*

500g  fresh angel-hair pasta
  ½ cup (125ml) olive oil
  2 birdseye chillies, seeded, chopped finely
  4 cloves garlic, crushed
  1 cup finely chopped fresh coriander leaves
  2 teaspoons salt
  2 tablespoons lemon juice
  ¾ cup (60g) parmesan cheese flakes

Cook pasta in large pan of boiling water, uncovered, until just tender; drain.

Meanwhile, heat oil in large frying pan; cook chilli and garlic, stirring, about 3 minutes or until fragrant. Remove pan from heat; stir in coriander and salt.

Gently toss coriander mixture with pasta and lemon juice in pan. Just before serving, sprinkle with cheese.

**SERVES 4**

Per Serving 34.8g fat; 3095kJ
Store Best made close to serving time.

# Warm pasta and lamb salad

**PREPARATION TIME** 20 minutes
**COOKING TIME** 25 minutes

500g lamb fillets, sliced thinly
   2 teaspoons olive oil
   3 teaspoons sugar
   ⅓ cup (80ml) lemon juice
   1 tablespoon dry red wine
   1 tablespoon mild sweet chilli sauce
   1 clove garlic, crushed
   2 tablespoons chopped fresh rosemary
   4 medium egg tomatoes (300g), quartered
500g spiral pasta
     olive oil spray
   ½ cup (125ml) beef stock
   2 tablespoons chopped fresh parsley
500g spinach, trimmed, chopped roughly

Combine lamb, oil, 1 teaspoon of the sugar, juice, wine, sauce, garlic and rosemary in bowl; turn to coat well.

Place tomatoes in single layer on oven tray, sprinkle with remaining sugar. Bake, uncovered, in moderate oven 20 minutes.

Meanwhile, add pasta to large pan of boiling water, boil, uncovered, until just tender; drain.

Drain lamb, reserving marinade. Coat non-stick pan with olive oil spray, add lamb in batches, cook until browned and tender. Return lamb to pan, add reserved marinade, stock and parsley, stir until mixture boils.

Gently toss with pasta, tomatoes and spinach.

**SERVES 6**

Per Serving 15.9g fat; 2141kJ
Store Lamb can be marinated several hours or overnight; keep, covered, in refrigerator. Tomatoes can be cooked 2 days ahead; keep covered, in refrigerator and reheat before adding to pasta.

# Spaghetti with seafood and herbs

**PREPARATION TIME** 10 minutes
**COOKING TIME** 20 minutes

| | |
|---|---|
| 375g | spaghetti |
| 1 | large carrot (180g) |
| 1/3 | cup (80ml) olive oil |
| 500g | uncooked shelled prawns |
| 150g | snow peas |
| 500g | scallops |
| 2 | cloves garlic, crushed |
| 1/3 | cup chopped fresh basil |
| 2 | tablespoons chopped fresh chives |
| 2 | teaspoons grated lemon rind |
| 1/3 | cup (80ml) lemon juice |
| 1 | teaspoon cracked black peppercorns |

Add pasta to large pan of boiling water, boil, uncovered, until just tender; drain.

Meanwhile, cut carrot into thin strips.

Heat oil in large frying pan or wok, add prawns, carrot, snow peas, scallops and garlic; stir-fry until seafood is tender. Add herbs, rind, juice and pepper; stir until well combined. Toss seafood mixture through hot pasta.

**SERVES 4**

Per Serving 21.1g fat; 2861kJ
Store Best made close to serving time.

# Spiced beef pasta salad

**PREPARATION TIME**
10 minutes (plus cooling time)
**COOKING TIME** 25 minutes

       1 tablespoon vegetable oil
  500g  minced beef
       1 teaspoon ground coriander
       1 teaspoon ground cumin
  1/4  teaspoon chilli powder
  1/2  teaspoon sweet paprika
       1 medium red capsicum (200g)
       1 medium yellow capsicum (200g)
  150g  green beans, chopped
  250g  penne
       2 teaspoons chopped fresh coriander

Dressing

       2 tablespoons light soy sauce
  1/4  cup (60ml) dry sherry
       1 tablespoon mirin
       1 tablespoon honey
       2 tablespoons tomato sauce

Heat oil in pan, add mince and spices, cook, stirring, until mince is browned; remove from heat, cool.

Quarter capsciums, remove seeds and membrane. Grill capsicum, skin side up, until skin blisters and blackens. Cover capsicum in plastic or paper for 5 minutes, peel away skin. Cut capsicum into strips.

Boil, steam or microwave beans until just tender, rinse under cold water; drain. Combine mince mixture, capsicum and beans in bowl.

Meanwhile, add pasta to large pan of boiling water, boil, uncovered, until just tender; drain. Combine mince mixture, pasta, coriander and dressing in bowl.

**Dressing** Combine all ingredients in jar; shake well.

**SERVES 4**

Per Serving 17.2g fat; 2206kJ
Store Salad can be made 3 hours ahead; keep, covered, in refrigerator.

# Macaroni cheese

**PREPARATION TIME** 15 minutes
**COOKING TIME** 30 minutes

*Use fresh or dehydrated peas and cook them before using, or use leftover cooked peas or thawed frozen peas. The heat from the sauce will be enough to tenderise frozen peas.*

| | |
|---|---|
| 1 | cup (180g) macaroni |
| 30g | butter |
| 2 | tablespoons plain flour |
| 2 | teaspoons dry mustard |
| 1½ | cups (375ml) milk |
| ¾ | cup (90g) grated cheddar cheese |
| 2 | hard-boiled eggs, quartered |
| ½ | cup (220g) peas |
| 2 | tablespoons chopped fresh parsley |

Add macaroni to large pan of boiling salted water, boil, uncovered, until macaroni is tender; drain.

Meanwhile, melt butter in large saucepan, stir in flour and mustard. Stir constantly over medium heat for 2 minutes or until mixture is bubbly; do not allow mixture to brown.

Remove from heat, gradually stir in milk. Return to heat, stir constantly over medium heat until the sauce boils and thickens slightly. Add cheese, stir until melted.

Gently stir in macaroni, eggs, peas and parsley. Serve immediately or place in heatproof dish, sprinkle top with a little extra cheese, place under hot grill for a few minutes or until lightly browned. You can also place mixture in ovenproof dish and bake, uncovered, in moderate oven for about 20 minutes or until lightly browned and heated through.

**SERVES 4**

Per Serving 21.3g fat; 1911kJ
**Store** This dish can be prepared up to 2 days ahead; keep, covered, in refrigerator.
**Microwave** Melt butter in large microwave-proof dish on HIGH for about 1 minute; stir in flour and mustard then milk gradually. Cook on HIGH, uncovered, for about 3 minutes or until mixture boils and thickens. Stir several times during the cooking. Add cheese, stir until melted, then add remaining ingredients.

# Spaghetti with tuna and olives

**PREPARATION TIME** 10 minutes
**COOKING TIME** 15 minutes

**375g spaghetti**
    **2 x 185g cans tuna in oil**
    **2 medium tomatoes (380g), chopped**
    **1/2 cup (60g) seeded black olives, halved**
    **3 teaspoons chopped fresh dill**
    **1/4 cup (60ml) bottled French salad dressing**

Add pasta to large pan of boiling water, boil,
uncovered, until just tender, drain. Return pasta
to pan with undrained tuna and remaining
ingredients, toss gently over heat until warm.

**SERVES 4**

**Per Serving** 26.3g fat; 2705kJ
**Store** Best made close to serving time. Or make it
several hours ahead and serve it cold.

# Penne boscaiola

**PREPARATION TIME** 10 minutes
**COOKING TIME** 15 minutes

*The quill-shaped penne is a good pasta to serve with a rich, substantial sauce like a boscaiola or carbonara because the ridges on each piece of pasta help 'trap' the creamy sauce and absorb its flavour.*

375g penne
1 tablespoon olive oil
1 large brown onion (200g), chopped finely
3 cloves garlic, crushed
4 bacon rashers, chopped finely
150g button mushrooms, chopped
300ml cream
1/2 cup (40g) coarsely grated parmesan cheese

Cook pasta in large pan of boiling water, uncovered, until just tender; drain.

Meanwhile, heat oil in large pan; add onion, garlic, bacon and mushrooms; cook, stirring, until onion is soft and browned lightly. Add cream to pan; stir until combined. Gently toss pasta and cheese in pan with mushroom cream sauce until heated through.

**SERVES 4**

**Per Serving** 42.7g fat; 3150kJ
**Store** Best made close to serving time.

# Seafood

# Crispy tuna with mint and chilli

**PREPARATION TIME** 20 minutes
**COOKING TIME** 10 minutes

650g tuna steaks
  2 tablespoons cornflour
  1/2 teaspoon Sichuan pepper
  2 tablespoons vegetable oil
  1 medium white onion (150g), sliced
  1 medium red capsicum (200g),
    thinly sliced
  1 medium yellow capsicum (200g),
    thinly sliced

1 cup (60g) firmly packed snow pea sprouts
1 tablespoon soy sauce
1 tablespoon mild sweet chilli sauce
1 tablespoon sake
1 tablespoon lime juice
2 teaspoons honey
2 tablespoons chopped fresh mint

Remove skin from tuna. Cut tuna into 3cm pieces, pat dry with absorbent paper. Toss tuna gently in combined cornflour and pepper, shake away excess flour.

Heat oil in wok. Add tuna in batches, stir-fry until just tender, remove; drain on absorbent paper.

Add onion and capsicums to wok, stir-fry until onion is soft. Add sprouts, sauces, sake, juice and honey, stir until hot.

Serve tuna over vegetable mixture; sprinkle with mint.

**SERVES 4**

Per Serving 19g fat; 1769kJ
Store Best made close to serving time.

# Salmon patties

**PREPARATION TIME** 25 minutes
**COOKING TIME** 10 minutes

> 5 medium potatoes (1kg), chopped
> 440g can salmon
> 1 stick celery (150g), finely chopped
> 1 small brown onion (80g), grated
> 1 small red capsicum (150g), finely chopped
> 1 tablespoon chopped fresh parsley
> 1 teaspoon grated lemon rind
> 1 tablespoon lemon juice
> 1/2 cup (75g) plain flour, approximately
> 1 egg, lightly beaten
> 2 tablespoons milk
> 1 cup (100g) packaged breadcrumbs, approximately
> 1 cup (70g) stale breadcrumbs, approximately
> oil for deep frying

Boil, steam or microwave potatoes until tender; drain well, place in medium bowl; mash until smooth.

Drain salmon well, remove skin and bones, add to potatoes in bowl, mash with fork, add celery, onion, capsicum, parsley and lemon rind and juice; mix well.

Divide salmon mixture evenly into 8 portions; a simple way is to form mixture into a big round and divide into 8 wedges. Shape each portion into a patty, dust with flour, shake away excess flour. Brush patties with combined egg and milk, toss in combined breadcrumbs; reshape if necessary while patting on the breadcrumbs.

Deep-fry patties, in batches, in hot oil for about 2 minutes or until golden brown and heated through. Drain on absorbent paper. Serve with lemon wedges.

**MAKES 8**

**Per Serving** 15.3g fat; 1383kJ
**Store** Patties can be prepared for frying up to a day ahead; keep, covered, in refrigerator.

# Baked fish with ginger and soy

**PREPARATION TIME** 10 minutes
**COOKING TIME** 25 minutes

**800g whole snapper**
- **1 tablespoon grated fresh ginger**
- **1 tablespoon peanut oil**
- **¼ cup (60ml) Chinese rice wine**
- **¼ cup (60ml) light soy sauce**
- **½ teaspoon sugar**
- **3 green onions, sliced thinly**

Cut three deep slits in each side of fish, place fish in oiled baking dish.

Rub ginger into fish; drizzle with combined oil, wine, sauce, and sugar. Bake, covered, in moderately hot oven about 25 minutes or until fish is cooked. Serve fish drizzled with some of the pan juices and topped with onion.

**SERVES 2**

**Per Serving** 11.6g fat; 1181kJ
**Store** Best made close to serving time.

# Smoked trout parcels with creamy dill sauce

**PREPARATION TIME** 20 minutes
**COOKING TIME** 15 minutes

- **12 leaves spinach**
- **2 large smoked trout (about 1.5kg)**
- **1 tablespoon drained capers, chopped**
- **4 sheets fillo pastry**
- **100g butter, melted**

**Creamy Dill Sauce**

- **$1/3$ cup chopped fresh dill**
- **$2/3$ cup (160ml) sour cream**
- **2 teaspoons horseradish cream**
- **2 teaspoons seeded mustard**

Add spinach to pan of boiling water, drain immediately, rinse under cold water, drain well; pat dry with absorbent paper.

Remove skin and bones from trout. Divide trout into 4 portions, top each with capers, wrap each portion in spinach leaves.

Cover fillo pastry with damp tea-towel to prevent drying out. Brush 1 fillo sheet with butter, cut lengthways into 3 equal pieces. Layer pieces at an angle on top of each other. Place 1 spinach-wrapped trout bundle in centre of fillo, gather edges together to form a parcel, brush with butter. Repeat with remaining fillo, butter and trout. Place parcels on greased oven tray. Bake, uncovered, in moderate oven about 15 minutes or until browned. Serve with Creamy Dill Sauce.

**Creamy dill sauce** Combine all ingredients in bowl; mix well.

**SERVES 4**

**Per Serving** 42.6g fat; 2313kJ
**Store** Recipe can be prepared 3 hours ahead.

# Cajun fish cutlets with tomato cucumber raita

**PREPARATION TIME** 10 minutes
**COOKING TIME** 10 minutes

*Cutlets of blue-eye (also known as trevalla) were used in this recipe.*

- 1 tablespoon Cajun seasoning
- 1 tablespoon plain flour
- 1 teaspoon ground cumin
- 4 white fish cutlets (1kg)
- 2 tablespoons lemon juice

### Tomato Cucumber Raita

- 200ml yogurt
- 3 Lebanese cucumbers (390g), seeded, chopped finely
- 2 medium tomatoes (380g), seeded, chopped finely
- 1 tablespoon lemon juice
- 1 teaspoon ground cumin

Combine Cajun seasoning, flour and cumin in small bowl; sprinkle over fish. Cook fish on heated oiled grill plate (or grill or barbecue) until browned both sides and cooked as desired.

Drizzle fish with lemon juice just before serving with Tomato Cucumber Raita.

**Tomato cucumber raita** Combine all ingredients in medium bowl.

**SERVES 4**

Per Serving 6.5g fat; 1187kJ
Store Best made close to serving time.

# Stir-fried spicy fish

**PREPARATION TIME** 10 minutes
**COOKING TIME** 10 minutes

400g  boneless white fish fillets
  1  teaspoon dried thyme leaves
  1  teaspoon dried parsley flakes
  2  teaspoons garlic salt
  1  teaspoon paprika
  1  teaspoon onion powder
  ½  teaspoon cracked black peppercorns
300g  baby yellow squash, sliced
150g  green beans, sliced
  1  tablespoon vegetable oil
 30g  butter
      few drops Tabasco sauce

Cut fish into 3cm pieces; pat dry with absorbent paper.

Add fish to combined herbs and spices; mix well.

Boil, steam or microwave squash and beans until just tender, drain immediately, rinse under cold water; drain.

Heat oil in wok. Add fish in batches, stir-fry until tender. Add squash, beans and butter, stir-fry until hot. Add Tabasco to taste.

**SERVES 4**

**Per Serving** 13.5g fat; 972kJ
**Store** Best made close to serving time.

# Tuna, bean and grilled vegetable salad

**PREPARATION TIME** 25 minutes
**COOKING TIME** 10 minutes

   1 **medium red capsicum (200g)**
   1 **medium yellow capsicum (200g)**
   1 **large brown onion (200g)**
   4 **large zucchini (600g)**
 1/3 **cup (80ml) olive oil**
200g **button mushrooms, halved**
400g **can cannellini beans, drained, rinsed**
425g **can tuna, drained, flaked**
 1/4 **cup (60ml) lemon juice**
   1 **clove garlic, crushed**
   1 **tablespoon finely chopped fresh parsley**

Quarter capsicums, remove and discard seeds and membranes. Roast under grill or in very hot oven, skin-side up, until skin blisters and blackens. Cover capsicum pieces with plastic or paper for 5 minutes, peel away skin; cut capsicum into thick strips.

Cut onion into 8 wedges; cut zucchini diagonally into 1cm-thick slices. Place onion and zucchini on oven tray; brush with 1 tablespoon of the oil. Grill onion and zucchini until browned lightly both sides.

Heat 1 tablespoon of the oil in small pan; cook mushrooms, stirring, until browned lightly.

Combine capsicum, onion, zucchini, mushrooms, beans and tuna in large bowl; gently toss with combined remaining oil, juice, garlic and parsley.

**SERVES 4**

Per Serving 31.2g fat; 1969kJ
Store Vegetables can be cooked up to 2 days ahead; store, covered, in refrigerator. Reheat or bring to room temperature before adding to tuna.

# Creamy fish and leek soup

**PREPARATION TIME** 20 minutes
**COOKING TIME** 10 minutes

| | |
|---|---|
| 50g | butter |
| 2 | medium leeks (700g), chopped coarsely |
| 4 | medium potatoes (800g), chopped coarsely |
| 1.5 | litres (6 cups) chicken stock |
| 1 | cup (250ml) milk |
| 250g | white fish fillets |

Heat butter in large pan; cook leek, stirring, until soft. Add potato and stock; simmer, covered, about 10 minutes or until potato is tender. Blend or process potato mixture, in batches, until smooth; return to pan.

Heat milk in small pan; cook fish, covered, over low heat, until cooked through. Drain over small bowl; reserve milk. Flake fish; discard any bones or skin. Add fish and milk to potato mixture; cook, stirring, until hot. Serve soup with toasted bread slices and snipped chives if desired.

**SERVES 4**

Per Serving 16.2g fat; 1653kJ
Store Potato and leek mixture can be made a day ahead; store, covered, in refrigerator.

# Easy Nicoise salad

PREPARATION TIME 10 minutes
COOKING TIME 0 minutes

125g  green beans
   2  x 425g cans tuna, drained
   1  large red oak leaf lettuce
410g  can bite-size potatoes, drained, quartered
250g  cherry tomatoes, halved
   1  cup (150g) black olives, seeded
  ½  cup (125ml) low-fat French dressing
   2  teaspoons seeded mustard
   1  clove garlic, crushed
   2  teaspoons fresh chervil leaves

Place beans in medium heatproof bowl, pour boiling water over beans, stand 5 minutes; drain. Rinse beans under cold water; drain well. Break tuna into large chunks.

Line large serving bowl with lettuce; top with combined beans, tuna, potatoes, tomatoes and olives. Mix dressing with mustard, garlic and chervil in small bowl, pour over salad.

## SERVES 6

Per Serving 16.3g fat; 1387kJ
Store Recipe can be prepared 3 hours ahead; store, covered, in refrigerator. Add tuna mixture to lettuce-lined salad bowl and pour over dressing just before serving.

# Baby octopus
# with snake beans

**PREPARATION TIME** 10 minutes
**COOKING TIME** 20 minutes

350g snake beans
500g baby octopus, cleaned
  2 tablespoons peanut oil
  1 medium red onion (150g),
    cut into wedges
  1 medium red capsicum (200g), sliced
  1 clove garlic, crushed
  2 tablespoons honey
  2 tablespoons balsamic vinegar
  2 tablespoons chopped fresh parsley

Place beans in medium heatproof bowl, pour boiling water over beans, stand 5 minutes; drain, keep warm. Cut octopus into quarters.

Heat half the oil in wok. Add octopus in batches, stir-fry until just tender, remove, keep warm.

Heat remaining oil in wok, add onion and capsicum, stir-fry until onion is soft; remove, keep warm. Add garlic, honey, vinegar and parsley to wok; stir-fry until hot.

Arrange beans on serving plates, top with capsicum mixture and octopus; drizzle with honey mixture. Sprinkle with extra parsley if desired.

**SERVES 2**

**Per Serving** 23.1g fat; 2598kJ
**Store** Prepared octopus, half the oil, garlic, honey, vinegar and parsley can be marinated in refrigerator up to 24 hours. Cook just before serving time.

# Spicy lemon seafood soup

**PREPARATION TIME** 15 minutes
**COOKING TIME** 35 minutes

500g  uncooked medium prawns
250g  white fish fillets
200g  calamari hoods
  2  teaspoons olive oil
  1  large red onion (300g), halved, sliced
  2  cloves garlic, crushed
1½  tablespoons grated lemon rind
  3  bay leaves
  1  teaspoon sweet paprika
  2  birdseye chillies, sliced
½  cup (125ml) dry white wine
¼  cup (60ml) lemon juice
  2  litres (8 cups) fish stock
  2  tablespoons roughly chopped fresh flat-leaf parsley
  2  green onions, chopped

Peel and devein prawns, leaving tails intact. Cut fish and calamari into 2cm pieces.

Heat oil in large pan, add red onion and garlic, cook, stirring, until onion is soft. Add rind, bay leaves, paprika, chillies, wine, juice and stock; simmer, uncovered, 20 minutes.

Add seafood, parsley and green onions, simmer, uncovered, 2 minutes or until seafood is just cooked; discard bay leaves.

**SERVES 6**

Per Serving 4g fat; 778kJ
Store Best made just before serving time.

# Salt and pepper butterflied prawns

PREPARATION TIME 30 minutes
COOKING TIME 10 minutes

    4 x 9cm square wonton wrappers
1kg uncooked medium prawns
    vegetable oil for shallow-frying
    1 tablespoon peanut oil
    2 cloves garlic, crushed
    1 birdseye chilli, sliced
    1 tablespoon lime juice
    2 tablespoons mild sweet chilli sauce
    3 green onions, sliced thinly
    2 teaspoons white sesame seeds, toasted

Seasoning

    1/2 teaspoon black peppercorns
    1/4 teaspoon coriander seeds
    3/4 teaspoon sea salt flakes
    1/4 teaspoon lemon pepper seasoning

Cut wonton wrappers in half diagonally. Shell prawns, leaving tails intact. Cut prawns down the back, cutting nearly all the way through; remove veins, flatten prawns slightly.

Shallow-fry wonton wrappers in hot oil, in batches, until lightly browned; drain on absorbent paper. Shallow-fry prawns in hot oil, in batches, about 30 seconds or until prawns are almost tender and have changed colour; drain on absorbent paper.

Heat peanut oil in wok or pan, add garlic and chilli, stir-fry until fragrant. Add prawns, juice, sauce and Seasoning, stir-fry until heated through. Stir in green onions, sprinkle with seeds. Serve with wonton wrappers.

**Seasoning** Lightly crush peppercorns and seeds, add salt and lemon pepper.

SERVES 4

Per Serving 6.5g fat; 682kJ
Store Best made just before serving time.

# Prawns with garlic herb butter

**PREPARATION TIME** 15 minutes
**COOKING TIME** 10 minutes

1kg  uncooked medium prawns
  2  tablespoons olive oil
  6  cloves garlic, crushed
50g  butter, chopped
  1  tablespoon lemon juice
1¹/₂  tablespoons chopped fresh parsley

Shell and devein prawns, leaving heads and tails intact.

Heat oil in large pan; cook garlic, stirring, until soft. Add prawns to pan, cook, turning gently, until prawns start to change colour and are almost cooked. Add butter and juice, cook, until prawns are just cooked through. Stir in parsley.

**SERVES 6**

**Per Serving** 13.5g fat; 803kJ
**Store** Best made just before serving time.

# Tuna and braised onion salad

**PREPARATION TIME** 10 minutes
**COOKING TIME** 30 minutes

  ¼ **cup (60ml) olive oil**
30g **butter**
  3 **large brown onions (600g), sliced**
  2 **tablespoons red wine vinegar**
  4 **tuna steaks (about 600g)**
120g **rocket**
325g **English spinach, shredded**

Heat oil and butter in heavy-base pan, add onions, cook, covered, stirring occasionally, about 20 minutes or until onions are very soft. Add vinegar, simmer, uncovered, 1 minute. Add tuna to same pan, cook, uncovered, until tuna is cooked as desired. Remove tuna from pan, cut into pieces. Serve warm tuna with braised onions, rocket and spinach.

**SERVES 4**

Per Serving 29g fat; 1980kJ
Store Onions can be cooked up to 3 days ahead; store, covered, in refrigerator. Cook tuna close to serving time.

# Baked rainbow trout with gremolata

**PREPARATION TIME** 5 minutes
**COOKING TIME** 30 minutes

4   **medium rainbow trout (1.6kg)**
2   **teaspoons olive oil**
2   **tablespoons lemon juice**
2   **tablespoons finely shredded flat-leaf parsley**
1   **clove garlic, crushed**
2   **teaspoons grated lemon rind**

Place fish in large oiled baking dish, pour juice over fish. Bake, uncovered, in moderate oven 25 minutes or until cooked through.

Combine parsley, garlic and rind in small bowl. Serve fish sprinkled with parsley mixture (gremolata).

**SERVES 4**

**Per Serving** 6.7g fat; 1265kJ
**Store** Best made close to serving time.

Platter, square dish and cutlery: *Empire Homewares*, Paddington; napkin: *The Bay Tree*, Woollahra

# Pan-fried fish with white wine sauce

**PREPARATION TIME** 5 minutes
**COOKING TIME** 25 minutes

*We used kingfish fillets for this recipe.*

- 1 **tablespoon butter**
- 1 **medium white onion (150g), chopped finely**
- ¹⁄₃ **cup (80ml) dry white wine**
- ¹⁄₂ **cup (125ml) cream**
- 1 **tablespoon coarsely chopped fresh chervil or parsley**
- 4 **small fish fillets (800g)**

Melt butter in small pan; cook onion, stirring, until soft. Add wine; simmer, uncovered, until wine is almost evaporated. Add cream; simmer, uncovered, until sauce thickens slightly. Stir in chervil or parsley just before serving.

Meanwhile, heat large oiled pan; cook fish until browned both sides and cooked through. Serve fish and sauce with potato chunks, if desired.

**SERVES 4**

Per Serving 22.2g fat; 1643kJ
Store Best made close to serving time.

# Tuna bean salad

**PREPARATION TIME** 15 minutes
**COOKING TIME** 0 minutes

100g mesclun lettuce
425g can tuna, drained, flaked
400g can butter beans, rinsed, drained
   1 small red onion (100g), sliced finely
250g yellow teardrop tomatoes
  1/2 cup (125ml) low-fat Italian dressing
   2 tablespoons coarsely chopped
     fresh parsley
   2 tablespoons coarsely chopped
     fresh basil leaves

Line 4 serving bowls with mesclun.

Combine tuna, beans, onion, tomatoes,
dressing, parsley and basil in large bowl;
divide among serving bowls.

**SERVES 4**

**Per Serving** 11.7g fat; 1021kJ
**Store** Best made close to serving time.

# Stir-fried calamari and chilli salad

**PREPARATION TIME** 10 minutes
**COOKING TIME** 10 minutes

- 4 medium calamari hoods (about 800g)
- 2 tablespoons olive oil
- 2 cloves garlic, crushed
- 1/2 teaspoon sambal oelek
- 1/2 teaspoon ground black pepper
- 1 tablespoon balsamic vinegar
- 2 teaspoons white wine vinegar
- 1 teaspoon sugar
  mixed salad leaves

Cut shallow diagonal slashes in criss-cross pattern on inside surface of calamari. Cut calamari into 6cm pieces.

Heat half the oil in wok. Stir-fry combined calamari, garlic, sambal oelek and pepper, in batches, until calamari is just tender.

Add remaining oil, combined vinegars and sugar, stir until hot.

Serve with mixed salad leaves.

**SERVES 4**

Per Serving 11.6g fat; 1035kJ
Store Best made close to serving time.

# Spicy tomato prawns

**PREPARATION TIME** 15 minutes
**COOKING TIME** 10 minutes

1 kg uncooked medium prawns
2 teaspoons hot paprika
1 teaspoon coriander seeds, crushed
1 teaspoon ground turmeric
1 teaspoon ground cumin
1 teaspoon cracked black pepper
1/4 teaspoon ground cloves
1/4 teaspoon ground cardamom
1/4 cup (60ml) water
1 tablespoon light olive oil
2 medium brown onions (300g), sliced
2 large tomatoes (500g), chopped
2 tablespoons finely chopped fresh
  coriander leaves

Shell and devein prawns, leaving tails intact.
Combine spices and water in small bowl.

Heat oil in pan, add onions, cook, stirring,
2 minutes. Add spice mixture, cook, stirring,
until fragrant.

Add prawns and tomatoes, cook, stirring,
until prawns have changed in colour and
are just tender. Remove from heat; stir in
fresh coriander.

**SERVES 4**

**Per Serving** 5.7g fat; 828kJ
**Store** Best made close to serving time.

# North African spiced fish with cucumber yogurt

**PREPARATION TIME** 10 minutes
**COOKING TIME** 8 minutes

*We used ling, also known as kingclip or rock ling, but use any firm, white fish you like.*

    1 **Lebanese cucumber (130g)**
    2 **teaspoons ground coriander**
    2 **teaspoons ground cumin**
    2 **teaspoons finely grated fresh ginger**
1/4 **cup (60ml) olive oil**
    4 **white fish fillets (800g)**
200ml **yogurt**
    2 **teaspoons finely chopped fresh mint leaves**
      **shredded lemon rind**

Grate cucumber coarsely; drain in sieve 5 minutes.

Meanwhile, combine coriander, cumin, ginger and oil in small bowl. Brush fish with spice mixture; cook fish on heated oiled grill plate (or grill or barbecue) until browned both sides and just cooked through.

Combine cucumber with yogurt and mint in small bowl; spoon over fish and sprinkle with lemon rind. Serve with salad if desired.

**SERVES 4**

Per Serving 20.1g fat; 1556kJ
**Store** Yogurt mixture can be made several hours ahead; store, covered, in refrigerator. Cook fish close to serving time.

# Vegetarian

# Red lentils and artichokes with capers

PREPARATION TIME 15 minutes
COOKING TIME 15 minutes

1½ cups (300g) red lentils
¼ cup (60ml) olive oil
 2 medium red onions (340g), sliced
 2 x 390g cans artichoke hearts,
   drained, halved
 2 cloves garlic, crushed
 2 tablespoons drained capers,
   finely chopped
 2 tablespoons chopped fresh parsley
¼ cup (30g) seedless black olives,
   finely chopped

 2 large tomatoes (500g), chopped
½ cup (125ml) water
¼ cup (60ml) tomato paste
 1 tablespoon red wine vinegar
 2 teaspoons sugar

Add lentils to large pan of boiling water; boil,
uncovered, about 8 minutes or until just
tender; drain; rinse, drain.

Heat half the oil in large frying pan, add
onions, cook, stirring, until just soft.

Add remaining oil, artichokes, garlic, capers,
parsley, olives and tomatoes; cook, stirring,
until combined.

Add lentils and remaining ingredients, stir
until hot.

SERVES 4

Per Serving 16g fat; 1716kJ
Store Recipe can be made a day ahead; store,
covered, in refrigerator.

# Vegetable soup with pistou

**PREPARATION TIME** 10 minutes
**COOKING TIME** 35 minutes

    1   small leek (200g), chopped finely
    1   medium carrot (120g), chopped finely
    1   small potato (120g), chopped finely
    1   small onion (80g), chopped finely
    1   small zucchini (90g), chopped finely
    1   small tomato (130g), chopped finely
    1   litre (4 cups) vegetable stock
  ¼   cup (45g) macaroni
300g   can cannellini beans, rinsed, drained

Pistou

  ¼   cup (20g) grated parmesan cheese
  ¼   cup chopped fresh basil leaves
    2   cloves garlic
  ¼   cup (60ml) olive oil

Combine leek, carrot, potato, onion, zucchini, tomato and stock in large saucepan. Bring to boil; simmer, covered, 20 minutes or until vegetables are tender.

Add macaroni, simmer, covered, 10 minutes. Add cannellini beans, simmer, uncovered, 5 minutes or until heated through. Just before serving, drop spoonfuls of Pistou into hot soup.

**Pistou** Blend or process all ingredients until smooth.

**SERVES 4**

Per Serving 16.8g fat; 1125kJ
Store Recipe can be made a day ahead; store soup and pistou separately, covered, in refrigerator.

# *Roasted vegetable salad*

**PREPARATION TIME** 15 minutes
**COOKING TIME** 20 minutes

    3  medium red capsicums (600g)
1kg  finger eggplants
  1/3  cup (80ml) olive oil
  1/3  cup (50g) chopped pistachios, toasted

**Yogurt Dressing**

    1  cup (250ml) plain yogurt
    1  clove garlic, crushed
  1/4  cup chopped fresh coriander leaves
1 1/2  tablespoons chopped fresh oregano
    1  teaspoon ground cumin
    2  teaspoons honey

Quarter capsicums, remove and discard seeds and membranes. Roast under grill or in very hot oven, skin-side up, until skin blisters and blackens. Cover capsicum pieces with plastic or paper for 5 minutes, peel away skin, slice capsicum thickly.

Cut eggplants in half lengthways. Heat 1 tablespoon of the oil in pan, add a quarter of the eggplants to pan, cook 10 minutes, or until browned all over and very soft; drain on absorbent paper. Repeat with remaining oil and eggplants.

Spread quarter of the Yogurt Dressing onto serving plate; top with a third of the eggplants, then a third of the capsicums. Repeat layering twice more. Top with remaining Yogurt Dressing; sprinkle with nuts.

**Yogurt dressing** Combine all ingredients in bowl; mix well.

**SERVES 6**

Per Serving 18.5g fat; 1025kJ
Store Capsicums, eggplants and Yogurt Dressing can be prepared a day ahead; store, covered, separately in refrigerator. Bring to room temperature before serving.

# Chickpea and rosemary soup

**PREPARATION TIME** 5 minutes
**COOKING TIME** 15 minutes

  2 tablespoons olive oil
  8 spring onions (200g), sliced
  2 cloves garlic, crushed
  2 tablespoons chopped fresh rosemary
425g can tomatoes
  3 cups (750ml) vegetable stock
300g can chickpeas, drained

Heat oil in large saucepan, add onions, garlic and rosemary; cook, stirring, until onions are soft.

Stir in undrained crushed tomatoes, cook, stirring, 5 minutes. Add stock and chickpeas, simmer, uncovered, about 5 minutes or until heated through.

**SERVES 4**

Per Serving 10.8g fat; 735kJ
**Store** Recipe can be made a day ahead; store, covered, in refrigerator.

# Tomato, fetta and spinach galettes

**PREPARATION TIME** 15 minutes
**COOKING TIME** 15 minutes

250g  frozen spinach, thawed
   2  sheets ready-rolled puff pastry
  1/3  cup (80ml) bottled pesto
200g  soft fetta cheese, crumbled
  1/4  cup finely chopped fresh basil leaves
250g  cherry tomatoes, halved
  1/4  cup (20g) coarsely grated
      parmesan cheese
   1  teaspoon cracked black pepper

Drain spinach then, using hands, squeeze excess liquid from spinach; chop roughly.

Oil 2 oven trays; place 1 sheet of pastry on each. Fold edges of pastry inward to form 1cm border; pinch corners of bases together.

Divide pesto between bases; spread evenly to cover base. Top each with spinach, fetta, basil and tomatoes; sprinkle with cheese and pepper. Cook in very hot oven about 15 minutes or until crisp and browned lightly.

**SERVES 4**

Per Serving 31.4g fat; 1599kJ
Store Best made close to serving time.

# Pesto pizzas

**PREPARATION TIME** 20 minutes
**COOKING TIME** 20 minutes

- ½ **cup (75g) pepitas**
- ¼ **cup firmly packed fresh basil leaves**
- ¼ **cup firmly packed fresh parsley sprigs**
- 1 **clove garlic, crushed**
- ¼ **cup (60ml) tomato puree**
- 1 **small kumara (300g)**
  **cooking-oil spray**
- 150g **button mushrooms, sliced**
- ½ **cup (60g) grated low-fat cheddar cheese**
- ½ **cup (50g) grated low-fat mozzarella cheese**
- ½ **cup (40g) grated parmesan cheese**
- 4 **small fresh or frozen pizza bases (wholemeal or plain)**

Add pepitas to dry pan, cook, stirring, over low heat about 5 minutes or until pepitas have popped; cool.

Process pepitas, herbs and garlic until combined. Gradually add puree while motor is operating.

Using a vegetable peeler, cut kumara into ribbons. Place pizza bases on oven trays that have been coated with cooking-oil spray.

Divide pepita pesto between pizzas, top with kumara and mushrooms, sprinkle with combined cheeses. Bake in moderately hot oven 20 minutes or until browned and crisp.

**SERVES 4**

Per Serving 26.3g fat; 4527kJ
Store Best made close to serving time.

# Leek and pumpkin fillo parcels

**PREPARATION TIME** 20 minutes
**COOKING TIME** 25 minutes

800g pumpkin, chopped
 30g butter
  2 medium leeks (700g), chopped coarsely
 3/4 cup (90g) coarsely grated cheddar cheese
  2 tablespoons seeded mustard
375g packet fillo pastry
 2/3 cup (160ml) vegetable oil

Boil, steam or microwave pumpkin until just tender; drain. Meanwhile, heat the butter in medium pan; cook leek, stirring, until soft. Combine pumpkin and leek in large bowl with cheese and mustard; mix well.

Cover fillo pastry with damp tea-towel to prevent drying out. Working with 3 fillo sheets at a time, brush each sheet lightly with oil; fold in half. Place 1/2 cup of vegetable mixture at one end of folded fillo; roll to enclose filling, folding in sides of fillo as you roll. Repeat with remaining vegetable mixture and fillo.

Place fillo parcels on oiled oven tray; brush lightly with oil. Bake, uncovered, in moderately hot oven about 20 minutes or until pastry is browned lightly. Serve with salad if desired.

**MAKES 8**

Per Serving 27g fat; 1747kJ
Store Pumpkin filling can be made 2 days ahead; store, covered, in refrigerator.

# Potato cakes with burghul salad

PREPARATION TIME 30 minutes
COOKING TIME 15 minutes

2 large old potatoes (600g), peeled, grated
3 green onions, chopped finely
1 egg yolk
1/4 cup (30g) soy flour
1 teaspoon ground coriander
vegetable oil for shallow-frying

Burghul Salad
1 medium yellow capsicum (200g)
1 medium red capsicum (200g)
1/3 cup (55g) burghul
1 1/2 cups finely chopped fresh parsley
1/3 cup (80ml) olive oil
1/4 cup (60ml) lemon juice

Dressing
1 cup (250ml) plain yogurt
2 teaspoons ground cumin
3/4 teaspoon ground turmeric
1 teaspoon sugar

Place potatoes between several sheets of absorbent paper, press paper to remove as much moisture as possible. Combine potatoes, green onions, egg yolk, flour and coriander in bowl.

Heat oil in pan, add 1/3 cup potato mixture in batches; flatten to 10cm rounds. Cook cakes slowly until browned underneath, turn, brown other side; drain on absorbent paper, keep warm. Serve topped with Burghul Salad; drizzle with Dressing.

**Burghul Salad** Quarter capsicums, remove seeds and membranes. Grill capsicums, skin-side up, until skin blisters and blackens; cool, peel away skin, chop capsicums finely.

Place burghul in small heatproof bowl, cover with boiling water, stand 20 minutes, drain. Place burghul between several sheets of absorbent paper, press paper to remove as much moisture as possible. Transfer burghul to bowl, add capsicums and remaining ingredients; mix well.

**Dressing** Combine all ingredients in bowl.

SERVES 6

Per Serving 21.9g fat; 1405kJ
Store Potato cakes are best made close to serving time. Burghul Salad and Dressing can be made a day ahead; store, covered, in refrigerator.

# Lentil and vegetable curry

**PREPARATION TIME** 10 minutes
**COOKING TIME** 30 minutes

1½ cups (300g) red lentils
1 tablespoon vegetable oil
1 large brown onion (200g),
  chopped coarsely
2 cloves garlic, crushed
3 teaspoons black mustard seeds
2 teaspoons cumin seeds
2 teaspoons ground turmeric
400g can tomatoes
3 cups (750ml) vegetable stock
1 medium carrot (120g), chopped coarsely
1 medium potato (200g), chopped coarsely
½ cup (125ml) coconut milk
½ cup (60g) frozen peas

Rinse lentils; drain. Heat oil in large pan; cook onion and garlic, stirring, until onion is soft. Add seeds and turmeric; cook, stirring, until seeds start to pop. Add undrained crushed tomatoes, stock, carrot, potato and lentils; simmer, covered, for about 20 minutes or until vegetables and lentils are just tender.

Just before serving, add milk and peas; stir over low heat until just hot. Serve with pappadums, if desired.

## SERVES 4

Per Serving 14.5g fat; 1747kJ
Store Vegetables and lentils can be cooked a day ahead; store, covered, in refrigerator or freeze. Reheat and add coconut milk and peas just before serving time.

# Char-grilled vegetables in mint vinaigrette

**PREPARATION TIME** 20 minutes
**COOKING TIME** 15 minutes

    3 medium red capsicums (600g)
    3 medium green zucchini (360g)
    3 medium yellow zucchini (360g)
    4 baby eggplants (240g)
    2 tablespoons olive oil
250g cherry tomatoes, halved

**Mint Vinaigrette**

    2 cloves garlic, crushed
    2 teaspoons cumin seeds, toasted
  1/2 cup (125ml) olive oil
    1 tablespoon lemon juice
    2 tablespoons red wine vinegar
    1 tablespoon shredded fresh mint

Quarter capsicums, remove and discard seeds and membranes. Roast under grill or in very hot oven, skin-side up, until skin blisters and blackens. Cover capsicum pieces with plastic or paper for 5 minutes; peel away skin, slice capsicums thickly.

Cut zucchini and eggplants lengthways into 1cm slices. Heat oil on grill plate (or grill or barbecue), cook zucchini and eggplants, in batches, until charred and cooked through; remove from pan. Add tomatoes to same pan, cook until just softened. Arrange vegetables on a plate and serve immediately, drizzled with Mint Vinaigrette.

**Mint vinaigrette** Combine all ingredients in jar; shake well.

**SERVES 4**

Per Serving 38.7g fat; 1728kJ
Store Vegetables best cooked just before serving time. Mint Vinaigrette can be made a day ahead; store, covered, in refrigerator.

# Mixed vegetable korma

**PREPARATION TIME** 10 minutes
**COOKING TIME** 20 minutes

- ¼ cup (60ml) korma paste
- 1 tablespoon black mustard seeds
- 1.5kg butternut pumpkin, chopped
- ⅓ cup (65g) red lentils, rinsed
- 2 cups (500ml) vegetable stock
- 500g cauliflower, chopped
- ½ cup (125ml) cream
- 200g baby spinach leaves

Cook paste and seeds in large heated dry pan until fragrant. Add pumpkin, lentils and stock, bring to boil; simmer, covered, 5 minutes. Add cauliflower; simmer, covered, about 10 minutes or until pumpkin is just tender, stirring occasionally. Add cream and spinach; stir until spinach just wilts.

**SERVES 4**

**Per Serving** 21.7g fat; 1639kJ
**Store** Recipe can be made 2 days ahead; store, covered, in refrigerator, or freeze for up to 2 months.

# Gazpacho celery salad

**PREPARATION TIME** 15 minutes
**COOKING TIME** 10 minutes

*You need a large bunch of celery (about 1.5kg) for this recipe.*

- ⅓ cup (65g) red lentils
- 1 Lebanese cucumber (130g)
- 125g rocket
- 1 cup (100g) walnuts, toasted
- 10 sticks celery (750g), trimmed, sliced finely
- 350g teardrop tomatoes, halved

### Gazpacho Dressing

- ½ cup (125ml) tomato juice
- 1 tablespoon olive oil
- 1 tablespoon chopped fresh dill
- 1 clove garlic, crushed
- 1 teaspoon sugar
- 1 teaspoon red wine vinegar
- ½ teaspoon Tabasco sauce

Rinse lentils under cold water; drain. Cook lentils in small saucepan of boiling water, uncovered, about 5 minutes or until just tender; drain, cool.

Halve cucumber lengthways, then slice finely. Combine lentils and cucumber slices with remaining salad ingredients in large bowl; gently toss with Gazpacho Dressing.

**Gazpacho dressing** Combine all ingredients in jar; shake well.

**SERVES 6**

Per Serving 15.2g fat; 865kJ
Store Salad best made close to serving time. Dressing can be made a day ahead; store, covered, in refrigerator.

# Rigatoni with tomato and avocado

**PREPARATION TIME** 15 minutes
**COOKING TIME** 15 minutes

500g rigatoni pasta
¼ cup (60ml) olive oil
400g can tomatoes, drained
  1 tablespoon tomato paste
  1 tablespoon lemon juice
  5 medium egg tomatoes (375g), seeded, chopped finely
  1 small red onion (100g), chopped finely
¼ cup coarsely chopped fresh parsley
  2 birdseye chillies, seeded, chopped finely
  1 clove garlic, crushed
¼ cup (40g) pine nuts, toasted
  1 cup (160g) Kalamata olives
  1 medium avocado (250g), chopped coarsely

Cook pasta in large pan of boiling water, uncovered, until just tender; drain. Transfer pasta to large bowl; stir in oil.

Meanwhile, blend or process tomatoes, paste and juice until smooth.

Combine tomato mixture and all remaining ingredients except avocado in large bowl. Add pasta and gently toss to combine. Stir avocado through just before serving.

**SERVES 4**

Per Serving 32.6g fat; 3235kJ
Store Best made close to serving time.

# Mulligatawny with pappadums

**PREPARATION TIME** 10 minutes
**COOKING TIME** 25 minutes

- 1 tablespoon vegetable oil
- 1 medium brown onion (150g), chopped coarsely
- 2 cloves garlic, crushed
- 1/4 cup (60g) mild curry paste
- 1 large apple (200g)
- 1 medium carrot (120g), chopped coarsely
- 1 medium potato (200g), chopped coarsely
- 1/2 cup (100g) red lentils
- 1 litre (4 cups) vegetable stock
- 1 tablespoon lemon juice
- 1/2 cup (65g) coconut milk powder
- 1 cup (250ml) water
- 1/4 cup (60ml) yogurt
- 8 pappadums
  vegetable oil, for deep-frying

Heat oil in large pan; cook onion and garlic, stirring, until onion is soft. Add paste; cook, stirring, until fragrant. Coarsely grate enough peeled, cored apple to make 2 tablespoons; reserve. Coarsely chop remaining apple; add to pan with carrot, potato, lentils and stock. Bring to boil; simmer, covered, 15 minutes or until lentils and vegetables are tender.

Blend or process mixture, in batches, until pureed. Return soup to pan, add juice and blended coconut milk powder and water; stir until hot. Sprinkle soup with reserved apple, drizzle with yogurt and serve with fried or microwaved pappadums.

Meanwhile, deep-fry pappadums, two at a time, in hot oil until puffed and crisp; drain on absorbent paper.

**SERVES 4**

**Per Serving** 27.2g fat; 1896kJ
**Store** Soup can be made to pureeing stage; store, covered, in refrigerator overnight or freeze. Reheat and add remaining ingredients just before serving.
**Microwave** Microwave pappadums, one at a time, on HIGH for 15 seconds on each side.

# Cabbage and zucchini stir-fry

**PREPARATION TIME** 10 minutes
**COOKING TIME** 10 minutes

- 1 tablespoon peanut oil
- 1 medium red onion (170g), sliced
- 2 medium zucchini (240g), sliced
- 1 large red capsicum (350g), sliced
- 300g Chinese cabbage, chopped
- 1/2 teaspoon dried crushed chillies
- 1 teaspoon fish sauce
- 1 tablespoon low-salt soy sauce
- 1/2 cup (125ml) vegetable stock
- 2 tablespoons brown malt vinegar
- 1/2 teaspoon brown sugar
- 1 cup (80g) bean sprouts
- 1/3 cup chopped fresh coriander leaves

Heat oil in wok or large frying pan, add onion, zucchini, capsicum and cabbage, stir-fry, until onion is soft.

Add chillies, sauces, stock, vinegar and sugar; cook, stirring, until mixture boils. Remove from heat, stir in sprouts and coriander; mix well. Serve with egg noodles if desired.

**SERVES 4**

Per Serving 5.2g fat; 424kJ
Store Best made close to serving time.

# Vegetable tagine

PREPARATION TIME 15 minutes
COOKING TIME 15 minutes

| | |
|---|---|
| 1 | tablespoon olive oil |
| 1 | medium brown onion (150g), chopped coarsely |
| 1 | clove garlic, crushed |
| 1½ | tablespoons ground cumin |
| 1 | tablespoon ground coriander |
| 2 | teaspoons caraway seeds |
| 2 | medium eggplants (600g), chopped |
| 1 | large zucchini (150g), chopped |
| 4 | medium tomatoes (760g), chopped |
| 300g | can chickpeas, drained, rinsed |
| 1 | tablespoon lemon juice |
| 1 | cup (250ml) vegetable stock |
| ⅓ | cup chopped fresh coriander leaves |

Heat oil in large pan; cook onion, garlic, spices, seeds and eggplant, stirring, until onion is soft. Add zucchini, tomato and chickpeas; cook, stirring, about 5 minutes or until vegetables are just tender.

Stir in juice and stock; cook, uncovered, until mixture boils and thickens. Just before serving, stir in coriander. Serve vegetable tagine with couscous, if desired.

**SERVES 4**

Per Serving 7.2g fat; 737kJ
**Store** Recipe can be made a day ahead; store, covered, in refrigerator or freeze. Reheat and stir in coriander just before serving.

# Tofu and vegetable stir-fry

**PREPARATION TIME** 15 minutes
**COOKING TIME** 15 minutes

350g cauliflower, chopped
350g broccoli, chopped
250g asparagus, sliced
350g green beans, sliced
   3 medium carrots (360g), sliced
  ¼ cup (60ml) olive oil
   2 cloves garlic, crushed
   1 tablespoon chopped fresh thyme
   1 teaspoon cracked black pepper
375g packet firm tofu, cubed
   2 medium brown onions (300g), sliced
250g button mushrooms, sliced
  ¼ cup (60ml) white wine
  ½ cup (125ml) vegetable stock
  ¼ cup (20g) grated parmesan cheese

Add cauliflower, broccoli, asparagus, beans and carrots to large pan of boiling water, boil 2 minutes, drain; rinse, drain.

Heat oil in wok. Add garlic, thyme, pepper and tofu, stir-fry until tofu is lightly browned, remove; keep warm.

Add onions and mushrooms to wok, stir-fry until onions are soft.

Add vegetable mixture, wine and stock and stir until sauce boils and thickens slightly. Stir in tofu.

Serve sprinkled with cheese.

**SERVES 6**

Per Serving 15.2g fat; 1082kJ
**Store** Best made close to serving time.

# Grilled haloumi, tomato and eggplant salad

**PREPARATION TIME** 15 minutes
**COOKING TIME** 15 minutes

 ½ **cup (125ml) olive oil**
 4 **baby eggplants (240g), sliced**
 4 **medium egg tomatoes (300g), halved lengthways**
400g **haloumi cheese, sliced thinly**
250g **rocket, chopped coarsely**
 ¼ **cup firmly packed fresh basil leaves**
 2 **tablespoons red wine vinegar**
 2 **teaspoons chopped drained capers**

Heat 1 tablespoon of the oil in large frying pan or grill plate; cook eggplant until browned both sides. Remove from pan.

Add tomato to same pan; cook, cut-side down, until browned and softened slightly. Remove from pan.

Heat another tablespoon of the oil in same pan; cook haloumi until browned lightly both sides.

Combine eggplant, tomato, haloumi, rocket and basil in large bowl with remaining oil, vinegar and capers.

**SERVES 4**

Per Serving 46.2g fat; 2234kJ
Store Best made close to serving time.

# Fast Salads

## Olive, onion and tomato salad

PREPARATION TIME 15 minutes
COOKING TIME 0 minutes

- 8  medium tomatoes (1.5kg)
- 1  large red onion (300g), sliced
- 2  cups (240g) seeded black olives
- 1  cup firmly packed fresh basil leaves, shredded

Dressing

- 1/4  cup (60ml) olive oil
- 1  tablespoon balsamic vinegar
- 1/2  teaspoon sugar
- 1  tablespoon Dijon mustard

Quarter tomatoes lengthways, remove seeds; slice each quarter in half lengthways. Combine tomatoes with remaining ingredients in bowl, add dressing; mix gently.

**Dressing** Combine all ingredients in jar.

SERVES 6

Per Serving 10.1g fat; 791kJ
Store Recipe can be prepared up to 2 hours ahead; store, covered, in refrigerator. Mix with dressing just before serving.

Olive, onion and tomato salad, Moroccan carrot salad (back)

## Moroccan carrot salad

PREPARATION TIME 15 minutes
COOKING TIME 0 minutes

- 3  large carrots (540g), grated
- 1/2  cup (115g) chopped fresh seeded dates
- 1/2  cup (70g) slivered almonds, toasted
- 1/4  cup chopped fresh coriander leaves
- 1/4  cup (60ml) olive oil
- 1/4  cup (60ml) white vinegar
- 2  teaspoons ground cumin
- 1  tablespoon honey

Combine carrots, dates, nuts and coriander in large bowl; gently toss with combined remaining ingredients.

SERVES 4

Per Serving 23.7g fat; 1332kJ
Store Recipe can be made 2 hours ahead.

# Eggplant, spinach and butter lettuce salad

PREPARATION TIME 10 minutes
COOKING TIME 10 minutes

      1 small eggplant (230g), sliced thinly
150g baby spinach leaves
      1 small butter lettuce, torn
      2 Lebanese cucumbers (260g), seeded, sliced finely
      2 green onions, shredded finely
   1/2 cup (125ml) oil-free Italian dressing

Place eggplant in single layer on oven tray; grill until lightly browned on both sides. Combine eggplant with remaining ingredients in large bowl

SERVES 4

Per Serving 0.5g fat; 243kJ
Store Best made close to serving time. Eggplant can be cooked a day ahead; store in refrigerator.

Coleslaw with fat-free dressing

# Coleslaw with fat-free dressing

PREPARATION TIME 20 minutes
COOKING TIME 0 minutes

300g cabbage, sliced
   1 large carrot (180g), grated coarsely
   4 green onions, sliced
   2 sticks celery (300g), sliced
1/4 cup (60ml) white wine vinegar
   2 tablespoons seeded mustard

Combine cabbage, carrot, onion and celery in large bowl. Combine vinegar and mustard in small bowl, pour over vegetables; toss well.

SERVES 4

Per Serving 0.5g fat; 159kJ
Store Recipe can be made 3 hours ahead; store, covered, in refrigerator.

Eggplant, spinach and butter lettuce salad

# Fast Vegetables

## Tri-fries with chilli salt

**PREPARATION TIME** 20 minutes
**COOKING TIME** 10 minutes

1 medium kumara (400g), unpeeled
1 medium white sweet potato (400g), unpeeled
2 medium new potatoes (400g), unpeeled
vegetable oil, for deep-frying
1½ teaspoons salt
¼ teaspoon hot chilli powder
¼ teaspoon freshly cracked black pepper

Scrub all potatoes; pat dry. Slice potatoes very thinly. Heat oil in large pan; deep-fry slices, in batches, until golden brown and crisp, drain on absorbent paper. Sprinkle hot fries with combined remaining ingredients and serve immediately.

**SERVES 6**

Per Serving 11.2g fat; 987kJ
Store Must be made just before serving time.

Bacon, buttermilk and chive mash

## Bacon, buttermilk and chive mash

**PREPARATION TIME** 10 minutes
**COOKING TIME** 15 minutes

2 bacon rashers
4 large potatoes (1.2kg), halved
½ cup (125ml) buttermilk
2 tablespoons finely chopped fresh chives

Discard fat from bacon, chop bacon finely. Heat small pan, cook bacon, stirring, until crisp; drain on absorbent paper.

Meanwhile, boil, steam or microwave potato until just tender; drain. Place potato in a large bowl, mash well; stir in bacon, buttermilk and chives.

**SERVES 4**

Per Serving 1.6g fat; 973kJ
Store Best made close to serving time.

# Rice and Noodles

# Coconut chicken soup (Tom kha gai)

**PREPARATION TIME** 15 minutes
**COOKING TIME** 30 minutes

- 1 litre (4 cups) chicken stock
- 1³/₄ cups (430ml) coconut milk
- ¹/₃ cup (80ml) lime juice
- ¹/₄ cup (60ml) fish sauce
- 1¹/₂ tablespoons finely chopped fresh lemon grass
- 6 kaffir lime leaves, torn
- 3 fresh coriander roots
- 1 teaspoon brown sugar
- 4 birdseye chillies, seeded, sliced
- 2 large chicken breast fillets (340g), sliced thinly
- 180g fresh egg noodles
- ¹/₃ cup loosely packed fresh coriander leaves

Add stock, milk, juice, sauce, lemon grass, lime leaves, coriander roots, sugar and half the chillies to large pan. Bring to boil; simmer, covered, 20 minutes. Discard coriander roots. Bring soup mixture to boil; stir in chicken and noodles. Bring to boil; simmer, covered, 1 minute. Ladle hot soup into serving bowls; sprinkle with coriander and remaining chilli.

**SERVES 4**

Per Serving 28.3g fat; 1827kJ
Store Best made close to serving time.

# Beef and snake beans with noodles

250g  rice vermicelli noodles
1½  tablespoons peanut oil
2  medium brown onions (300g), sliced
2  tablespoons red wine vinegar
1  tablespoon brown sugar
600g  beef eye-fillet, sliced thinly
2  teaspoons grated fresh ginger
3  cloves garlic, crushed
¼  cup (60ml) hoisin sauce
2  tablespoons salt-reduced soy sauce
2  tablespoons chopped fresh
coriander leaves
350g  snake beans, chopped
1  tablespoon white sesame seeds

Place noodles in heatproof bowl, cover with boiling water, stand 5 minutes, drain.

Heat 1 teaspoon oil in wok or large frying pan, add onions, vinegar and sugar, cook over low heat, stirring occasionally, until onions are caramelised; remove.

Heat all but 1 teaspoon oil in wok, add beef in batches, stir-fry until browned and tender; remove from pan.

Heat remaining teaspoon of oil in wok, add ginger, garlic, sauces, coriander, beans and seeds, stir-fry until beans are just tender. Return beef and onions to wok with noodles, stir until heated through.

**SERVES 4**

Per Serving 17.6g fat; 2306kJ
Store Best made close to serving time.

# Hokkien noodles with fried tofu and prawns

**PREPARATION TIME** 20 minutes
**COOKING TIME** 15 minutes

|       |                                      |
|------:|--------------------------------------|
|     5 | dried shiitake mushrooms             |
|  500g | hokkein noodles                      |
|  300g | packet firm tofu                     |
|       | vegetable oil, for deep frying       |
|     1 | tablespoon peanut oil                |
|     2 | cloves garlic, crushed               |
|     2 | teaspoons grated fresh ginger        |
|  500g | large uncooked prawns, shelled       |
|   1/3 | cup (80ml) oyster sauce              |
|     2 | tablespoons light soy sauce          |
|     1 | tablespoon hoisin sauce              |
|     1 | tablespoon rice vinegar              |
|  300g | baby choy sum, chopped               |
|     2 | tablespoons sweet chilli sauce       |
|     2 | tablespoons fresh coriander leaves   |

Place mushrooms in small heatproof bowl; cover with boiling water. Stand 20 minutes; drain. Discard stems; slice caps thinly. Rinse noodles under hot water; drain. Transfer to large bowl; separate noodles with a fork.

Cut tofu into 2cm cubes. Heat vegetable oil in wok or large frying pan. Deep-fry tofu, in batches, until browned all over; drain on absorbent paper. Heat peanut oil in same cleaned wok or large frying pan; stir-fry garlic, ginger and prawns until prawns just change in colour. Add noodles, mushrooms, sauces and vinegar; stir-fry until heated through. Add choy sum; stir-fry until just wilted. Serve noodles topped with tofu, chilli sauce and coriander leaves.

**SERVES 4**

Per Serving 22.8g fat; 1925kJ
Store Best made close to serving time.

# Risotto Milanese with lamb

**PREPARATION TIME** 5 minutes
**COOKING TIME** 40 minutes

    1 litre (4 cups) lamb or beef stock
    1 cup (250ml) dry red wine
    1 cup (250ml) water
    $^1/_3$ cup (80ml) olive oil
  500g lamb strips
    3 cloves garlic, crushed
    1 large onion (200g), chopped finely
  200g Swiss brown mushrooms, sliced thinly
    $^1/_2$ teaspoon saffron threads
    2 cups (400g) arborio rice
    $^1/_2$ cup (60g) coarsely grated cheddar cheese

Creamed Mushroom Sauce

  20g butter
  200g button mushrooms, sliced
    $1^1/_2$ tablespoons lemon juice
300ml cream

Combine stock, wine and water in large pan; bring to boil, then simmer.

Meanwhile, heat half the oil in medium frying pan; cook lamb, in batches, stirring until browned all over and cooked through. Cover to keep warm.

Heat remaining oil in same pan; cook garlic, onion, mushrooms and saffron, stirring, until onion is soft. Add rice, stir to coat in oil mixture. Stir in 1 cup hot stock mixture; cook, stirring, over low heat until liquid is absorbed. Continue adding stock mixture, in 1-cup batches, stirring, until absorbed between each addition. Total cooking time should be about 35 minutes or until rice is just tender. Gently stir in lamb and cheese; serve with Creamed Mushroom Sauce.

**Creamed mushroom sauce** Heat butter in medium pan; cook mushrooms, stirring, until browned. Stir in juice and cream. Bring to boil; simmer, stirring, about 3 minutes or until sauce thickens slightly.

**SERVES 4**

Per Serving 70g fat; 5030kJ
Store Risotto best made close to serving time. Sauce can be made 2 days ahead. Reheat without boiling.

# Singapore noodles

**PREPARATION TIME**
10 minutes (plus standing time)
**COOKING TIME** 15 minutes

- 1/3 cup (40g) dried shrimp
- 400g rice vermicelli noodles
- 3 eggs
- 1/4 cup (60ml) peanut oil
- 1 large onion (200g), sliced coarsely
- 2 teaspoons grated fresh ginger
- 1 small red capsicum (150g), sliced
- 120g Chinese barbecued pork, chopped
- 1/2 cup (60g) frozen peas
- 2 tablespoons curry powder
- 1 tablespoon light soy sauce
- 1 teaspoon sesame oil
- 1/2 cup (125ml) vegetable stock
- 2 cups (160g) bean sprouts
- 4 green onions, sliced
- 1 tablespoon chopped fresh coriander leaves

Place shrimp in heatproof bowl, cover with boiling water, stand 20 minutes; drain. Place noodles in separate heatproof bowl, cover with boiling water, stand 5 minutes; drain.

Whisk eggs in small bowl until frothy. Heat 1 tablespoon of the peanut oil in wok or large pan, add egg mixture, stir until just cooked, remove, cover to keep warm.

Heat remaining peanut oil in wok, add onion and ginger, cook, stirring, until fragrant. Add capsicum and pork, stir-fry 2 minutes. Add shrimp, noodles, peas, curry powder, sauce, sesame oil, stock, sprouts and green onions, stir until heated through. Add egg and coriander, mix gently.

**SERVES 4**

Per Serving 25.5g fat; 2650kJ
Store Best made close to serving time.

# Smoked salmon, avocado and udon salad

**PREPARATION TIME** 10 minutes
**COOKING TIME** 15 minutes

250g udon noodles
300g sliced smoked salmon
 90g snow pea sprouts
  2 tablespoons chopped fresh chives
  1 small red onion (100g), chopped finely
  2 small avocados (400g), chopped finely
 1/3 cup (80ml) light olive oil
  2 tablespoons seasoned rice vinegar
  1 tablespoon mirin
  1 tablespoon lime juice
  2 teaspoons wasabi

Cook noodles in large pan of boiling water, uncovered, until just tender; drain. Rinse under cold water; drain.

Separate smoked salmon slices; cut into small strips. Just before serving, gently toss noodles and salmon in large bowl with sprouts, chives, onion, avocados and combined remaining ingredients.

**SERVES 4**

Per Serving 52.1g fat; 3257kJ
Store Best made close to serving time.

# Asparagus and oregano barley risotto

**PREPARATION TIME** 25 minutes
**COOKING TIME** 35 minutes

- ¼ cup (50g) pearl barley
- 1 large red capsicum (350g)
- 750g asparagus, chopped
- 1 teaspoon olive oil
- 1 small leek (200g), chopped
- 1 clove garlic, crushed
- ¼ cup chopped fresh oregano
- 2 cups (400g) arborio rice
- 2 cups (500ml) water
- ½ cup (125ml) dry white wine
- 1 litre (4 cups) chicken stock
- ½ teaspoon ground nutmeg
- ⅓ cup (25g) grated parmesan cheese
- 1 teaspoon freshly ground pepper

Add barley to large pan of boiling water, boil, uncovered, 20 minutes or until tender; drain.

Meanwhile, quarter capsicum, remove and discard seeds and membranes. Roast under grill or in very hot oven, skin-side up, until skin blisters and blackens. Cool, peel, slice capsicum. Boil, steam or microwave asparagus until just tender; drain, rinse, drain.

Heat oil in pan, add leek and garlic, cook, stirring, until leek is soft. Add oregano and rice, stir until combined.

Combine water, wine and stock in separate pan, bring to boil, keep hot. Stir ½ cup (125ml) hot stock mixture into rice mixture, cook, stirring, over low heat until liquid is absorbed.

Continue adding stock mixture, in 1-cup batches, stirring, until absorbed between each addition. Total cooking time should be about 30 minutes or until rice is just tender.

Stir in barley, capsicum, asparagus and remaining ingredients; stir until hot.

**SERVES 6**

**Per Serving** 3.6g fat; 1464kJ
**Store** Best made close to serving time. Barley can be cooked a day ahead; store, covered, in refrigerator.

# Sesame chicken noodle salad

**PREPARATION TIME** 10 minutes
**COOKING TIME** 25 minutes

680g  chicken breast fillets, sliced
   1  clove garlic, crushed
   2  tablespoons sweet chilli sauce
$\frac{1}{2}$  teaspoon sesame oil
$\frac{1}{4}$  cup (60ml) rice vinegar
   2  tablespoons soy sauce
   1  tablespoon lemon juice
   1  green onion, sliced finely
   2  teaspoons sugar
600g  fresh egg noodles
   1  medium yellow capsicum (200g)
   1  large carrot (180g)
200g  watercress, trimmed
   1  tablespoon peanut oil
250g  asparagus, trimmed, halved
   2  teaspoons white sesame seeds, toasted

Combine chicken, garlic and chilli sauce in large bowl.

For dressing, combine sesame oil, vinegar, soy sauce, juice, green onion and sugar in jar.

Cook noodles in large pan of boiling water, uncovered, until just tender; drain.

Discard seeds and membranes from capsicum, cut capsicum and carrot into long thin strips. Combine noodles, capsicum, carrot and watercress in large serving bowl.

Heat peanut oil in wok or large pan; stir-fry chicken mixture, in batches, until browned and tender. Add asparagus to wok, stir-fry until just tender.

Combine chicken and asparagus with noodle mixture, drizzle with dressing, sprinkle with sesame seeds.

## SERVES 6

**Per Serving** 10.9g fat; 1502kJ
**Store** Best made close to serving time. Chicken can be marinated several hours or overnight.

# Sausage risotto

**PREPARATION TIME** 10 minutes
**COOKING TIME** 35 minutes

500g beef sausages
  4  small tomatoes (520g)
  2  tablespoons olive oil
  1  large leek (500g), chopped coarsely
  1  clove garlic, crushed
¼  cup (60ml) dry red wine
  2  cups (400g) calrose rice
  2  litres (8 cups) boiling beef stock
½  cup (40g) grated parmesan cheese
  1  tablespoon finely chopped fresh parsley

Cook sausages in heated oiled pan until browned all over and cooked through; slice thickly.

Meanwhile, cut tomatoes into wedges; place wedges on oven tray, brush with half the oil. Bake tomato in moderate oven about 15 minutes or until softened.

Heat remaining oil in large pan; cook leek and garlic, stirring, until leek is soft. Add wine; simmer until liquid is reduced by half. Stir in rice and stock; simmer, uncovered, stirring occasionally, about 25 minutes or until most of liquid is absorbed and rice is just tender. Just before serving, stir in sausages, tomato, cheese and parsley.

**SERVES 4**

**Per Serving** 46g fat; 3850kJ
**Store** Best made close to serving time. Sausages and tomatoes can be cooked a day ahead; store, covered, in refrigerator.

# Honeyed scallop and chilli stir-fry

**PREPARATION TIME** 10 minutes
**COOKING TIME** 10 minutes

600g fresh egg noodles
  3 teaspoons peanut oil
  1 medium onion (150g), quartered
  2 medium red capsicums (400g), sliced thinly
  1 large stick celery (100g), sliced
100g snow peas
200g scallops
  1 tablespoon honey
  1 teaspoon chilli sauce
  2 teaspoons chopped fresh mint

Cook noodles in a large pan of boiling water, uncovered, until just tender; drain.

Meanwhile, heat oil in wok, add vegetables to pan, stir-fry over high heat for 1 minute. Add scallops, honey, chilli sauce and mint to pan, stir-fry for about 2 minutes or until scallops are tender. Add noodles; toss well.

**SERVES 4**

**Per Serving** 5g fat; 1333kJ
**Store** Best made close to serving time

Fork and plate: *Empire Homewares*, Paddington

**Horseradish cream** a creamy, prepared paste of grated horseradish, vinegar, oil and sugar.

**Horseradish relish** made from seasonal root vegetables, horseradish oil and vinegar; used as an accompaniment to roasted and grilled meat.

**Korma paste** a commercially made mild curry paste.

**Lamb**
*Eye of loin* a cut from a row of loin chops, with the bone and fat removed.
*Fillet* tenderloin; small piece of meat from row of loin chops or cutlets.
*Minced* also known as ground lamb.

**Mango chutney** commercially packaged product based on mango and various spices; traditionally served with Indian food, but is also good with cold meats, salads or cheese.

**Mexibeans** is the trade name for canned pinto beans in chilli sauce.

*Mexibeans*

**Milk evaporated skim** canned product available in supermarkets.

**Mirin** a sweet, low-alcohol rice wine used in Japanese cooking; sometimes referred to simply as rice wine but should not be confused with sake, the Japanese rice wine made for drinking.

**Mushrooms**
*Oyster* also called abalone mushrooms, they are grey-white in colour and shaped like a fan.
*Shiitake* cultivated mushroom with a rich, meaty flavour; available fresh and dried. Dried shiitake mushrooms should be reconstituted before using by soaking in boiling water.

*Straw* available canned in brine.
*Swiss brown* also known as Cremini mushrooms; light to dark brown in colour with a mild, earthy flavour.

**Mustard**
*Dijon* a pale brown, distinctively-flavoured, fairly mild French mustard.
*French* smooth, sweet mustard made with mustard seeds, malt vinegar, caramel, herbs and spices.
*Seeded* also known as wholegrain; French-style coarse-grained mustard made from crushed mustard seeds and Dijon-style French mustard. The seeds can be black or yellow.

**Noodles**
*Bean thread vermicelli* also known as cellophane noodles; made from green mung bean flour. Good softened in soups and salads or deep-fried with vegetables.
*Udon* thick Japanese noodles; can be round, square or flat and made from either wheat or corn flour. Available fresh or dried.

**Oil**
*Olive oil spray* available from supermarkets in aerosol cans.
*Sesame* made from roasted, crushed white sesame seeds; a flavouring rather than a cooking medium.
*Olive paste* black prepared, bottled product made from black olives and olive oil; available in delicatessens and some supermarkets.

**Onion**
*Brown* also known as yellow; pungent flesh adds flavour to a vast range of dishes.
*Green* also known as scallion or, incorrectly, shallot; an immature onion picked before the bulb has formed, having a long, bright-green edible stalk.
*Red* also known as Spanish, red Spanish or Bermuda onion; a sweet-flavoured, large, purple-red onion that is particularly good eaten raw in salads.
*White* interchangeable with brown onions; pungent flesh adds flavour to a vast range of dishes.

*pancetta*

**Paprika** packaged powder made by grinding aromatic sweet red pepper pods. The two blends available are Hot, which is fiery, and Sweet, which is mild.

**Pancetta** an Italian salt-cured pork roll, usually cut from the belly; used, chopped, in cooked dishes to add flavours. Bacon can be substituted.

**Pepitas** dried and hulled pumpkin seeds available from supermarkets.

**Pepper, lemon** a packaged blend of crushed black peppercorns, lemon, herbs and spices.

**Polenta** a flour-like cereal made from ground corn (maize); similar to cornmeal, but finer. Also the name of the dish made from it.

**Pumpkin** member of the gourd family; also known as squash.
*Butternut* pear-shaped with golden skin and orange flesh.

**Redcurrant jelly** a preserve made from redcurrants; used as a glaze for desserts and meats, or in sauces.

**Sake** Japan's favourite rice wine is used in cooking, marinating and dipping sauces. If sake is unavailable, dry sherry, vermouth or brandy can be used as a substitute. To consume as a drink, it should be served warm: stand container of sake in hot water for 20 minutes.

**Salmon roe** bright red salmon eggs; served in sauces, salads and as a spread or dip.

**Salt, garlic** packaged blend of salt and ground, dehydrated garlic, available in supermarkets.

**Sambal oelek** (also ulek or olek) Indonesian in origin; a salty paste made from ground chillies.

**Sauce**

*Fish* also known as nam pla or nuoc nam; made from salted, pulverised, fermented small fish, often anchovies. Has pungent smell and strong taste; use sparingly.

*Oyster* Asian in origin, this rich, brown sauce is made from oysters and their brine, cooked with salt and soy sauce, then thickened with starch.

*Satay* commercially prepared spicy sauce, originating in South-East Asia, based on peanuts and a variety of herbs and spices.

*Sweet chilli* relatively mild, Thai-type sauce made from red chillies, sugar, garlic and vinegar.

*Tabasco* brand name of an extremely fiery sauce made from vinegar, hot red peppers and salt.

*Teriyaki* a sauce consisting of soy sauce, corn syrup, vinegar, ginger and spices; also the name of a distinctive glaze on grilled meats.

**Sausages**

*Italian-style* made from coarsely ground pork and pork fat, flavoured with garlic.

**Sichuan pepper** also known as Chinese pepper; small, red-brown aromatic seeds, resembling black peppercorns in size and shape, with a peppery lemon flavour.

*Sichuan peppercorns*

*sumac*

**Snake beans** long (40cm), thin, round green beans; Asian in origin.

**Snow pea sprouts** see bean sprouts.

**Soup, condensed tomato** commercially made concentrated soup, available in supermarkets.

**Spinach** also known as English spinach; delicate crinkled green leaves on thin stems. Good eaten raw in salads or steamed gently on its own. The green vegetable often mistakenly called spinach is correctly known as silverbeet, Swiss chard or seakale.

**Star anise** a dried, star-shaped pod whose seeds have an astringent aniseed flavour.

**Sugar, brown** an extremely soft, finely granulated sugar retaining molasses for its characteristic colour and flavour.

**Sumac** a purple-red, astringent spice ground from berries growing on shrubs that flourish wild around the Mediterranean; it adds a tart, lemony flavour to dips and dressings and goes well with barbecued meat.

**Sun dried tomatoes** halved, dehydrated tomatoes available loose (by weight), in packets, and bottled in oil.

**Sun-dried tomato paste** commercially produced paste made from sun-dried tomatoes, oil, garlic, basil, salt, pine nuts and spices; available in delicatessens and some supermarkets.

**Taco seasoning** a packaged seasoning made from oregano, cumin, chillies and other spices.

**Tomato**

*Pasta sauce* prepared, bottled sauce of crushed tomatoes and various spices and herbs.

*Paste* triple-concentrated tomato puree used to flavour soups, stews and sauces.

*Puree* canned, pureed tomatoes (not tomato paste). Substitute with fresh peeled and pureed tomatoes.

**Vietnamese mint** not a mint at all, this narrow-leafed, pungent herb, also known as Cambodian mint, daun laksa and laksa leaf, is widely used in South-East Asian soups and salads.

**Vinegar, white wine** vinegar made from white wine.

**Water chestnuts** crunchy, nutty-tasting tuber with brownish-black skin and white flesh; available fresh or canned.

**Water spinach** a long-leafed dark green vegetable. Cook in the same way as spinach, or add to stir-fries and soups. The stems can be split lengthways and soaked in cold water to make them curl.

# Index